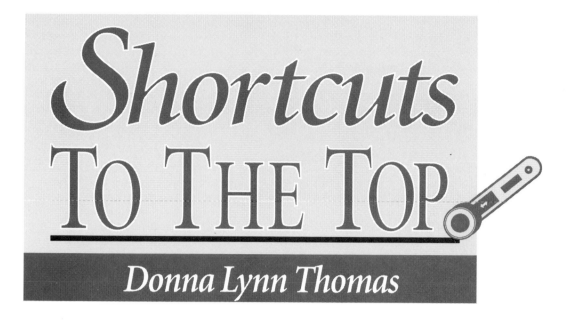

Shortcuts
TO THE TOP

Donna Lynn Thomas

That Patchwork Place®

Acknowledgments

Shortcuts to the Top was a big undertaking, and the bigger the project, the more people there are to thank for all their help; no one does it alone.

First, I want to thank all the pattern testers. Their work helps ensure the accuracy of the patterns; their corrections and suggestions are extremely important. Many thanks to Donna Nagle, Kay Kolditz, Kari Lane, Dee Glenn, Nancy Sullivan, Char Mulyca, Julie Miran, Ann Richardson, Robin Chambers, Gabriel Pursell, Pam Sutey, Deb Rose, Tamie Renbarger, Roxanne Carter, and Mildred Gerdes.

None of my quilts would be finished if not for the work of some wonderful quilters. Their beautiful hand and machine quilting brought life to my quilt tops and ease to my life. Every time UPS arrived with a finished quilt, I was astounded at the beauty of the quilting. Each of these ladies is a true artist with the needle, so many thanks to Aline Duerr and her sister Norma Jean Rohman, Ann Woodward, Roxanne Carter, Kari Lane, and Maureen McGee.

Several quilters were gracious enough to contribute quilts for this book. Some of their beautiful quilts are pattern models, and others are interesting variations. Many thanks to Donna Nagle, Kari Lane, Pam Sutey, Deb Rose, Tamie Renbarger, and Roxanne Carter.

A great big thank-you goes to a group of quilters from the Prairie Quilt Guild in Wichita, Kansas. These ladies contributed fabric toward my Birds in the Air quilt. Thank you to Teresa Mulhern, Leslie Snodgrass, Kay Ehlen, Beth Tanner, and Mary Ann Gertsen.

One last thank-you goes to my dear friend in Texas, Susan Stamilio. She brainstormed with me over some design elements, and as a result, "Susan's Southern Star" was named for her.

Dedication

This book is dedicated to the three wonderful men in my life—Terry, Joe, and Pete. Terry, as always, is my sounding board, editor, and panic-control guy, not to mention the best friend and husband imaginable. Joe and Pete gave me computer time along with hugs, kisses, and uncomplaining help when needed. I love you guys—even more than quilting.

I'd also like to dedicate this book to my dear, sweet mother-in-law for her love, support, and typing expertise. Her much-needed support is always freely given.

Last but not least, I dedicate a good chunk of the proceeds from this book to my sons' orthodontist. (Tee-hee, I couldn't resist that one!)

Credits

Editor-in-Chief .... Barbara Weiland
Technical Editors .... Ursula Reikes
　　　　　　　　　　　　　　　　　　Susan I. Jones
Managing Editor .... Greg Sharp
Copy Editor........................... Liz McGehee
Proofreader............................ Tina Cook
Text and Cover Design .... Kay Green
Production .... Kathleen Darcy
Photography............................ Brent Kane
Illustration and Graphics .... Karin LaFramboise
　　　　　　　　　　　　　　　　　　Laurel Strand

Shortcuts to the Top ©
© 1994 by Donna Lynn Thomas

That Patchwork Place, Inc.
PO Box 118, Bothell
WA 98041-0118
USA

Printed in the United States of America
99 98 97 96 95 94　　6 5 4 3 2 1

Thomas, Donna Lynn,
　　Shortcuts to the top/Donna Lynn Thomas
　　　　p. cm.
　　　ISBN 1-56477-057-5 :
　　　1. Patchwork—Patterns. 2. Machine quilting—Patterns.
　　3. Cutting. I. Title.
TT835.T455 1994　　　　　　　　　　94-6364
746.9'7—dc20　　　　　　　　　　　　CIP

Contents

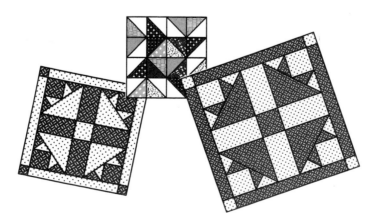

Introduction

Men and women have always led busy lives. Whether we are married or unmarried, have children or not, or work inside or outside the home, we wear many hats in our families and the community. In our ever-dwindling leisure time, many of us find pleasure in a craft or hobby—needlework, gardening, painting, woodworking, or some other form of creative expression. It's a need as old as mankind.

For those of us who love the art of quiltmaking, there is an increasing buffet of different techniques that fall into the category of quiltmaking. There truly is something to suit everyone's interest.

One of the newer approaches to quiltmaking is the marriage of rotary cutting and machine piecing. It fills the bill for many quiltmakers who are short on time or simply cannot or do not wish to hand-piece. Many longtime quilters have switched to rotary cutting and machine piecing on account of arthritis or other disabilities. Others, like myself, use these techniques because of the tremendous accuracy and precision that they provide.

This book was written as a companion to my previous books, *Shortcuts: A Concise Guide to Rotary Cutting* and *A Perfect Match: A Guide to Precise Machine Piecing*. In the following pages, you will find patterns and directions for making fifteen quilt designs using rotary-cutting and machine-piecing techniques.

The book is divided into four sections, each focusing on a different technique. Each section builds on the technique presented in the previous section, so you can learn and progress at your own pace, or review and begin at your current skill level.

The book begins with basic cutting and piecing techniques along with general information on equipment, supplies, fabric preparation, and pressing. Section I introduces the concept of straight-grain strip piecing, while Section II takes it one step further with bias strip piecing. Section III explains more exciting uses for bias strip piecing, as introduced in *Shortcuts*. The last skills section presents the piecing skills required for cutting and sewing more complex designs with diamonds, set-in seams, and curves.

Each pattern section begins with a small warm-up project to help you master the skills presented. The patterns that follow are arranged from the easiest to more challenging. All of these things help to make *Shortcuts to the Top* a "user-friendly" book. In the final chapter, you will find general directions for finishing your quilt.

I encourage you to read the basic information in the front of this book in its entirety, whether you are a beginner or not. There are many equally wonderful ways to achieve the same results with quiltmaking, and different methods appeal to different people. Quiltmaking techniques are similar to a buffet dinner—you try a little of everything to decide what you like best, and you end up with an array on your plate different from everyone else's. When it comes to quiltmaking, my method may very well differ from yours. It's always a good idea to read and be aware of these different approaches so that you may either try them or account for their differences when you make one of the quilts in the book.

As you make your favorite quilts in *Shortcuts to the Top*, I think you'll agree that we've seen only the tip of the iceberg when it comes to rotary-cutting techniques. Maybe you'll discover some of your own shortcuts for making topnotch quilt tops!

General Information

EQUIPMENT AND SUPPLIES

Basic Supplies

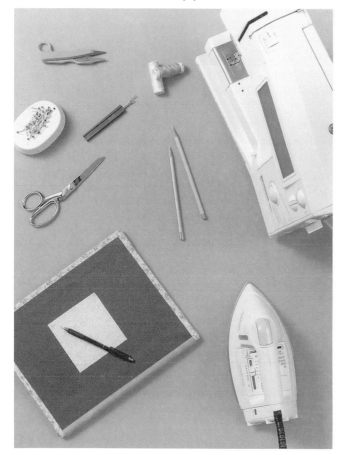

Sewing Machine. You need a simple straight-stitch sewing machine in good working order to piece a quilt top. Make sure that the machine is clean and has been professionally serviced so that the thread tension is properly adjusted and there are no mechanical problems. Use a size 80/12 needle and replace it with each new quilt or when you hear a popping noise every time the needle pierces the fabric. Set your machine at about 12 stitches per inch.

Thread. I prefer 100% cotton thread with a silk finish, although I have lived in places where it was not readily available. Cotton-covered polyester is an adequate substitute. For general sewing, I use a gray thread that is no darker than the darkest fabric, and no lighter than the lightest. If there are a lot of cream-based prints in the quilt, I use a cream or natural-colored thread. The idea is to avoid thread show-through at seam intersections. This won't be a problem if your machine's tension is properly adjusted, your seams are evenly distributed at intersections, and you press the seam allowances to set the stitches. Thread for hand sewing the binding to the quilt backing should match the binding fabric color as closely as possible.

Regular Sewing Supplies. Items, such as a good set of fabric shears, silk pins, thread clips, and sewing needles, should be part of your basic sewing kit. Use your fabric shears for fabric only. Invest in good-quality silk pins. Thread clips are small scissors that are useful for clipping threads and doing close work. I use my quilting "between" needles for most hand stitching, such as slipstitching binding.

Seam Ripper. This item is essential for "reverse stitching," when it is necessary to undo and restitch a seam for accuracy.

Pencils. You need a fine-line mechanical or #2 lead pencil. Colored pencils are useful for marking on a busy print, where a lead pencil won't show. Keep pencils sharp for accuracy.

Sandpaper Board. This is an invaluable tool for accurately marking fabric. You can easily make one by adhering very fine sandpaper to a hard surface, such as wood, cardboard, poster board, or a self-sticking needlework mounting board. The sandpaper grabs the fabric and keeps it from slipping as you mark.

Ironing Equipment. Good ironing supplies need not be fancy, just clean and operable. Use a traditional ironing board or a terry cloth towel on a heat-resistant surface. A steam iron set for cotton is best.

Keep the iron clean, following the manufacturer's instructions. Use only distilled water, especially if you have hard water. It's nice if your iron has a spray feature, but a spray bottle works as well. Do not use the same spray bottle on your fabrics that you use for any household chemicals.

Rotary Equipment

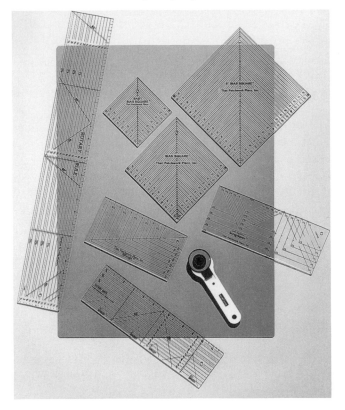

Rotary Cutter. A rotary cutter looks like a pizza cutter with a protective shield for the blade. There are many brands and styles available. Generally, the large cutter is better for precisely cutting through several layers of fabric. The small cutter is great for miniatures, and the curved-handle cutters are wonderful for those with arthritis or other hand/wrist ailments. The major consideration when selecting a cutter is safety.

Rotary cutters have extremely sharp blades. Handle them with care. Never leave the blade exposed, even for a minute. It's too easy to brush your hand against an open blade on your work table, causing a nasty wound. Cutters with manually engaged safety shields are the safest. It is important to keep the screw on the back of the cutter tight enough so that the shield cannot slip away from the blade. Properly tightened, the blade shield protects you and others from the blade's sharp edge. Cutters with automatically retracting shields are not as safe as those with manual shields because the automatic shields retract when dropped on your foot or pressed against your fingers, arms, or hands.

Rotary Mat. You need a specially designed rotary mat to use with your rotary cutter. If you try to cut on any other surface, you will ruin not only the cutting surface but also the cutting blade. I have mats in several sizes, with and without printed grid lines. My favorite mats have lines spaced 1" apart with ⅛" marks on the outer edges. They also have assorted angle lines. The large mat stays on my work table; I use smaller mats for workshops and classes. Store mats flat and avoid extreme hot or cold temperatures that can cause warping. Heat from a hot mug or high-intensity work lamp is enough to damage them. (Personal experience taught me both of these lessons!) There is no way to fix a warped mat.

Rotary Rulers. A good rotary ruler is an invaluable tool and an absolute necessity for rotary cutting. The assortment and variety of rulers available today can be overwhelming. Buy a ruler with the following features:

- Choose rulers made of hard, ⅛"-thick acrylic plastic. It is too easy to cut into and ruin a soft, flexible ruler.
- Look for rulers marked horizontally and vertically in ⅛" increments. This is particularly important because ⅛" increments are used in many quilt patterns.
- Select a ruler with 30°, 45°, and 60° lines. The corner of the ruler is the 90° guide.

The most frequently asked question when shopping for a ruler is, What size ruler should I buy? There is no perfect answer. No one size fits all cutting situations. The most versatile size is probably the 6" x 12" ruler, but there are reasons to have an assortment of sizes on hand.

The 3" x 18" ruler is wonderful for a lot of routine cutting and measuring that does not require the width of a 6"-wide ruler. The 18" length is also nice for cutting bias strips.

The 6" x 24" ruler is cumbersome, unless you prefer to work with fabric folded only once. It is a wonderful ruler, however, for cutting longer bias strips, trimming borders and the sides of a finished quilt top, or for cutting away excess batting and backing in preparation for binding the quilt.

I would never be without my 1" x 6" ruler. I keep it right by my sewing machine so I can quickly check the accuracy of my work as I stitch.

Another ruler I have found to be a treasure is the 15" square ruler. It is wonderful for cutting larger pieces of fabric to make strip sets, and it makes cutting large squares for side setting triangles a snap. It is also great for squaring up the corners of a quilt before adding borders.

There are also quite a number of specialty rulers, designed to accompany some very clever timesaving techniques. The only one you need for making the quilts in this book is the Bias Square® ruler, which is used in conjunction with the bias strip–piecing methods. However, you may want Judy Hopkins's ScrapMaster (formerly ScrapSaver) ruler, which simplifies resizing or cutting single triangles from scraps.

FABRICS

Selecting Fabric

Choosing fabrics is an individual thing. Some of us have trouble choosing dark fabrics or working with pastels. Still others have a lot of difficulty with one particular color family. Scrap or multi-fabric quilts seem to make a lot of people uneasy. I work mostly by instinct, but I can offer you a few tricks I use to choose fabrics for my quilts. I view fabric choices in three varieties: planned, color-family scrap, and contrast scrap.

A planned quilt is one in which a limited number of prints are chosen and used in exactly the same places throughout the quilt design. Usually, I begin with one "anchor" fabric. It is generally, although not always, a multicolor print that I'd like to use as the focal point of the quilt, either as a border or background print or as the main draw within the blocks.

Next, I identify the other colors in the print. The color circles on the selvages of some fabrics can help you with this step. Decide which colors you want to use and where to place them in the design.

Having made these choices, I go to my fabric stash and start pulling prints in the chosen colors. As you use this method, remember to vary the type and scale of the prints you choose, to keep the quilt interesting. Don't be afraid to mix geometric prints, small and large florals, swirly prints, splashy and quiet prints, and plaids or checks. Also, if you find you don't have enough of one print, switch gears and choose a couple of prints that work equally well; use them randomly in place of the one print. A good example of a planned quilt is "Cross-Eyed Puss" on page 17. There are two different light pinks in that quilt because I didn't have enough of the one pink that I was absolutely dying to use!

A color-family scrap quilt is one in which a color family is assigned to a particular place in the quilt or quilt block. Then, a wide variety of prints within that color family are chosen and used randomly in the assigned position. "Mosaic Sparkler" on page 24 is an excellent example. The color families are teal and violet with assorted prints of both for the lights.

Sometimes, I combine elements of both methods by planning most of the prints but assigning a color family to just one or two positions. "Susan's Southern Star" on page 21 was completely planned, except for the gold star, which I thought would twinkle a little better if I used a variety of prints.

A contrast quilt is lots of fun. Assign dark and light values to each position in the design and then work with all kinds of color families that meet the contrast requirements. "Birds in the Air" on page 22 is a very simple example of a contrast quilt. This quilt sparkles because of the wide leeway allowed in identifying dark and light from block to block. The medium print used as the light in one block could be the dark in another and vice versa. You can also work with shades of light and dark within one color family. This is called a monochromatic color scheme. The red "Checkerboard Chain" on page 19 is an example of a monochromatic color scheme.

Preparing Fabric

It's a good practice to check all of your fabrics separately for bleeding before prewashing them. Place a 4" swatch of each fabric in a jar of very hot water. For fabric scraps or fat quarters (18" x 22" pieces of fabric), I test the whole piece in the sink rather than cut it up. Let it soak for about twenty minutes. If the water is clear, the fabric is ready to use. If the water is colored, rinse the fabric several times until the water is clear. If it does not stop bleeding after a few rinses, I recommend that you do not use the fabric in your quilt.

Prewashing fabric is a subject of much discussion among quilters. Generally, prewashing accomplishes several things; it preshrinks fabrics, removes any excess dye, and removes the sizing and mildew retardant added by the manufacturer. In order to retain the mildew resistance, I do not prewash fabrics until I am ready to use them.

If you choose to prewash, use warm water and wash different colors separately. Dry on low heat or air fluff until damp dry. Gently press the fabric with a hot iron. Use a spray of water to ease out any stubborn creases and refold carefully.

BASIC CUTTING

After prewashing and pressing, you are ready to cut the pieces for your quilt. Basic rotary-cutting directions follow. Refer to *Shortcuts* for in-depth information on rotary-cutting techniques.

Lay the freshly pressed fabric on the rotary mat with the fold toward you, the raw edges to the left, and the selvages at the top of the mat. (If you are left-handed, place the raw edges to the right.) Bring the fold to the selvage edges for a second fold if you are working with a 12"-long ruler.

Straighten the cutting edge first to ensure straight fabric strips. Lay your rotary ruler just inside the raw edges of all fabric layers at the left-hand edge. Lay one edge of the Bias Square ruler on the bottom fold of the fabric and adjust the straight ruler so that it is flush with the Bias Square. Hold the straight ruler securely in place. Anchor it by placing your fingers or the palm of your hand on the mat, to the side of the ruler.

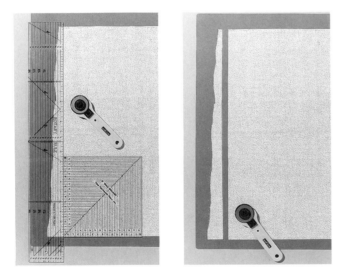

Cut away from yourself with firm, downward pressure as the blade rolls along the ruler's edge. Make one clean, firm cut from the fold to the selvages. It may be necessary to slowly and carefully "walk" your hand up the ruler as you cut. Be careful not to shift the ruler out of line. Cut completely past the selvages and avoid the urge to roll the cutter back and forth in a short, choppy fashion. This makes a ragged, inaccurate edge. If you find you are not cutting through all layers, exert a stronger downward pressure or check the blade for nicks or dulling. This first cut is your straight-grain cutting edge.

Cutting Strips

Almost all rotary cutting begins with strips of fabric, which are then cut into other shapes, such as squares, triangles, rectangles, and diamonds. For example, if you need a 2½"-wide strip, align the 2½" line of your ruler with the clean-cut, left-hand edge of the fabric. To prevent a "bent" strip, always align one of the ruler's horizontal lines with the fold at the bottom edge of the fabric. This ensures an exact right-angle cut. Always cut strips ½" wider than the desired finished size to allow for two ¼"-wide seams. Remove selvages from all strips before using them.

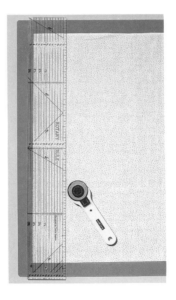

Cutting Squares

Cut fabric into strips the measurement of the square. If you need 2⅞" squares that finish to 2⅜", cut a 2⅞"-wide strip. Then, crosscut 2⅞" squares from the strip, working from left to right. Be sure to align a horizontal line of the ruler or Bias Square ruler across the bottom of the strip before each cut.

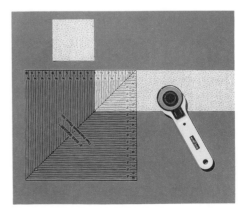

Cutting Half-Square Triangles

Make half-square triangles by cutting a square once diagonally, so the straight grain is on the two short edges. When used in a block, the short edges fall at the outside edges of the block.

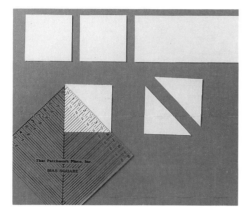

To determine the size square needed to yield two half-square triangles, including seam allowances, determine the desired finished size of the short (straight-grain) edge of the triangle. Add ⅞" to this figure and cut a square this size. When cut diagonally, the square yields two half-square triangles with the proper seam allowances included.

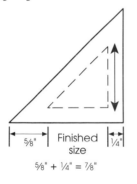

⅝" | Finished size | ¼"

⅝" + ¼" = ⅞"

Cutting Quarter-Square Triangles

Make quarter-square triangles by cutting a square twice diagonally, so the straight grain is on the long edge in each resulting triangle. When positioned in a block, this long edge is along the outer edge of the block as in the Ohio Star pattern.

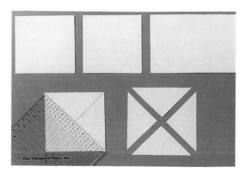

To compute the size square needed for a quarter-square triangle, determine the desired finished size of the long (straight-grain) edge of the triangle. Add 1¼" to this measurement and cut a square this size. This size square, when cut twice diagonally, will yield four triangles with the proper seam allowances included.

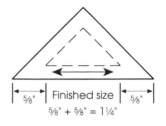

⅝" | Finished size | ⅝"

⅝" + ⅝" = 1¼"

Cutting Triangles for Diagonally Set Quilts

Quarter-square triangles are generally used for the side setting triangles at the outer edges of diagonally set quilts. The correct size to cut the side setting triangles is given in the quilt plans, but you may want to know how to calculate the size if you make changes in the quilt dimensions. When setting blocks on the diagonal, you only know the finished size of the short edge of the side setting triangle, which is equal to the finished size of the quilt block. To cut quarter-square triangles, you need to know the finished size of the triangle's long edge. To figure this measurement, multiply the length of the finished short edge by 1.414. Round up the result to the nearest ¼" and add 1¼" to this figure to determine the size of the square to cut for side setting triangles. The triangles will be slightly oversized, but that's OK. Simply trim back the edges before adding the borders. (See page 94.)

For example, a quilt made with 7" square finished blocks, set on the diagonal, requires that the short side of the side setting triangles finishes to 7". Multiply 7" by 1.414 to find the finished size of the triangle's long edge (7" x 1.414=9.898"). Round up 9.898" to the nearest ¼" (10") and add 1¼" to equal 11¼". Cut one 11¼" square for every four side setting triangles you need.

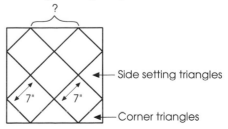

The corner triangles of diagonally set quilts require a similar calculation. Half-square triangles are used so that the corners are on the straight grain. The known measurement is the finished size of the long edge (the finished block size). To find the dimension of the short edge, multiply the long edge by .71 and round up to the nearest ¼". Add ⅞" to this figure to compute the size of the square.

Using the same example as above, multiply 7" by .71. This equals 4.97". Round this figure up to 5" and add ⅞". Cut one 5⅞" square for every two corner triangles you need.

Cutting Bars and Rectangles

A true rectangle is twice as long as it is wide, such as 2" x 4" or 3" x 6". Bars are simply stretched squares of any other dimension. For either shape, cut the strips ½" wider than the finished width to allow for the seam allowances. Then cut the bars or rectangles from the strip in the same manner you cut squares from strips.

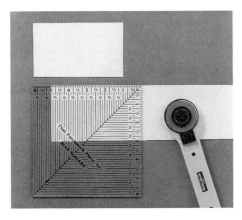

Cutting Large Pieces

When you need to cut large pieces of fabric for side setting triangles, it's handy to have a 15"-square ruler. If you don't have one or you need to cut larger pieces, you can use the rulers you have on hand.

Prepare your fabric for cutting by creating a straight-grain cut edge as shown on page 8. Lay the long edge of your ruler even with the fold, measuring the required distance from the clean-cut edge. Place a ruler line along the straight-grain edge to ensure that you are creating a right angle with the ruler. Cut along the short edge of the ruler, perpendicular to the fold.

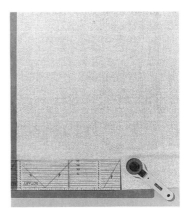

Turn your ruler, aligning the long edge with the short cut you just made. Be sure that a horizontal line on the ruler matches the fold to ensure a right-angle cut. Continue the cut up to the selvage edges.

You are now ready to cut this piece into squares, rectangles, or whatever other shapes you need.

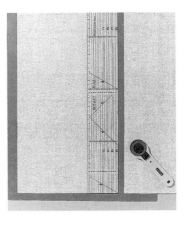

Nubbing Triangles

Nubbing triangle points removes excess fabric that extends past the ¼"-wide seam allowances, so that the edges of squares and triangles are easier to match for more accurate stitching. Even when sewing triangles to triangles, nubbing eliminates the need to go back and clip off the "dog ears" that remain after sewing a seam.

Nubbing before sewing ensures better matching.

To nub half-square triangles:

Add ½" to the finished dimension of the triangle's short side. To nub a 1½" finished-size, half-square triangle, place the Bias Square ruler on the triangle at the 2" mark as shown in the diagram (1½" + ½" = 2").

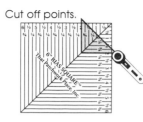

Cut off points.

Half-Square Triangle

To nub quarter-square triangles:

1. Add ⅞" to the finished size of the triangle's long edge and measure this distance from the left corner toward the right. Cut the excess fabric to the right of the ruler edge.
2. Add ½" to the finished size, turn the triangle over, and measure this distance from the first nub to the right. Cut the excess fabric to the right of the ruler edge. For example, to nub a 4¼" finished-size, quarter-square triangle, nub first to 5⅛" (4¼" + ⅞" = 5⅛") and second to 4¾" (4¼" + ½" = 4¾").

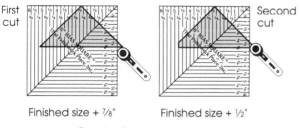

First cut · Finished size + ⅞"　　Second cut · Finished size + ½"

Quarter-Square Triangle

Resizing Half-Square Triangles

Sometimes you may need to cut a few more triangles than you could cut from a strip of fabric. Rather than cutting another strip, cut extra triangles from leftover fabric, or resize waste triangles from strip units.

1. Create a square corner on the straight grain of a fabric piece, using the corner of your ruler.

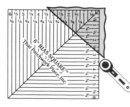

Square off the corner of edge triangle.

2. Add ½" to the desired finished size of the triangle's short side. Position the Bias Square

on the corner of the scrap at these markings and cut away the excess fabric extending past the ruler sides.

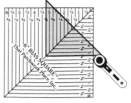

Nub the triangle points.

3. Rotate the triangle and cut the long edge to ¼" from the nubbed corners. The triangle is now cut and nubbed to fit your requirements.

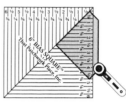

Trim excess.

Note: Judy Hopkins's ScrapMaster (formerly ScrapSaver) ruler is a useful tool for performing these functions without calculations. Be sure to follow the package directions.

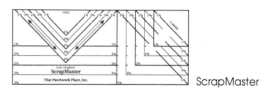

ScrapMaster

Reusing Large Leftover Pieces

Larger pieces of fabric can also be used to cut extra strips.

To cut strips from square or rectangular pieces:

1. Use a large square ruler to make a squared-off corner with two clean-cut adjacent edges.

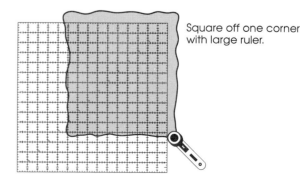

Square off one corner with large ruler.

If you do not have a square ruler, cut one edge on the straight of grain. Cut the adjacent edge, making sure a horizontal line on the ruler lies along the first clean-cut edge.

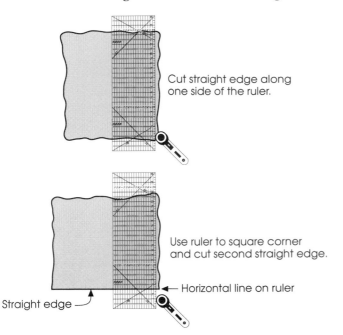

Cut straight edge along one side of the ruler.

Use ruler to square corner and cut second straight edge.

Horizontal line on ruler

Straight edge

2. Cut the fabric into strips as usual, then cut the strips into the shapes you need.

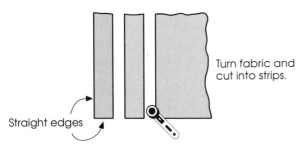

Turn fabric and cut into strips.

Straight edges

To cut strips from triangular pieces:

1. Square off two adjacent edges to create a straight-grain corner in the same manner described above.

Square up corner of triangle.

2. Cut the triangle into fabric strips and then into the shapes you need.

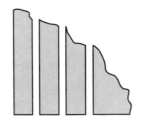

Cut into strips, then into other shapes.

PRESSING

There are two primary reasons for pressing seams in a particular direction: 1) so that the seams rest against each other (butt) at the intersections for sewing, and 2) so your completed block or quilt will lie flat and smooth. Pressing toward the darker fabric, which is a common direction in quiltmaking, is a luxury you can consider after these two conditions are met.

There are pressing instructions with each quilt plan in this book. Arrows shown in the illustrations indicate the direction to press the seams, to ensure that the block goes together easily.

In quilt blocks where intersecting seams do not butt together easily, you have some options:

1. Flip one of the seams so it butts at the intersection and let the seam allowance twist from one side to the other in the middle of the seam. This is unconventional, but it is important to butt the seams for accurate stitching and a smooth, flat intersection. The twist in the middle of the seam can usually be mashed flat with a bit of spray and a good pressing. This is my first choice of all the pressing options.

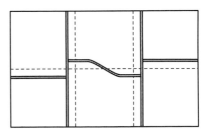

Flip seam so intersection butts exactly.

2. Press both seams open and pin them to match. The intersection will be flat, and both seams will have a half twist. There is, however, the potential for batting or thread to show through at the open seams. Without a ridge of butting seams, your seams may slip away from each other. Despite these potential problems, this method is my second choice.

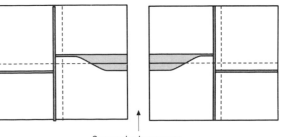

Seam to be sewn.

3. Open the seam allowance on one of the seams and match the intersection with pins. This trick softens the twist in the middle of the seam by eliminating one layer and avoids having all four layers of the two seams facing in one direction at the intersection.

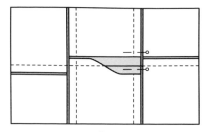

Partially flipped seam.

4. The least desirable option is to leave both seams pressed as they are and pin carefully. The bulge at the intersection may cause the points to shift or result in a large lump when sewn.

Refer to my book *A Perfect Match* for more detailed information on creating pressing plans for future projects.

Pressing Tips

There are a few tips for pressing a seam crisply toward one side, without any pleats or puckers showing on the right side.

1. Press, don't iron. Pressing is the gentle lowering, pressing, and lifting of the iron along the length of a seam. Moving the iron forcefully back and forth along the seam distorts it. Use heat, steam, and an occasional spritz of water to press the fabric in the desired direction.

2. Always press the seam line flat after sewing, before pressing it in one direction or the other. This relaxes and sets the thread, eases out any puckers resulting from stitching, and smooths out any fullness you may have purposely eased in as you stitched. Try this and you'll be surprised at how smoothly and easily the seam will turn as you press it to one side.

3. Press from the right side. Use the tip of the iron to gently press the top fabric over the seam allowance.

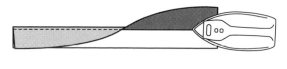

4. Press in the direction of the fabric's straight grain. When the straight grain lies along the seam, gentle pressing along the seam follows the straight grain. With seams that are sewn on the bias edge, press at a 45° angle to the seam along the straight grain. Don't press along the bias seam itself.

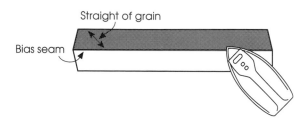

5. Correct pressing mistakes by returning the unit to its original unpressed position and steaming the seam. Then press again in the correct direction.

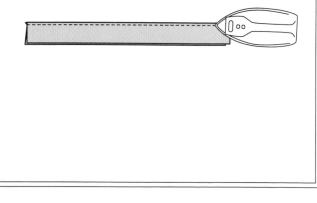

STITCHING

Sewing an Accurate Seam Allowance

With rotary cutting, ¼"-wide seam allowances are included in all cutting dimensions. Therefore, it is imperative to sew an accurate seam. Otherwise, the impact of minute errors in the seam width increases with each subsequent seam.

Most people assume that the right-hand edge of the standard presser foot is the ¼" seam guide for their sewing machine. This is not necessarily so. Many machines are close, but close is not good enough if you want your pieces to fit together without a lot of fuss and bother, especially when using rotary-cutting techniques. It is very important to test your seam guide for accuracy by conducting a strip test.

1. Cut three strips of fabric, each 1½" x 3".
2. Sew the strips together carefully, using the edge of your presser foot or a designated ¼" guide on the throat plate of your machine. After sewing and pressing, the center strip should measure exactly 1" wide.

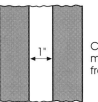

Center strip should measure a perfect 1" from seam to seam.

If the center strip does not measure exactly 1" wide, you must adjust the guide on your machine. My classroom experience has shown that most seams that are sewn using the edge of the presser foot or the seam guide on the throat plate as a guide are slightly wider than ¼". Most often, the finished center strip measures ⅞". To create a new guide, you can try using a different presser foot or needle position. Zigzag machines with five needle positions usually stitch an accurate ¼"-wide seam when the needle is moved one notch to the right of the center position and the edge of the presser foot is used as a guide. Do another strip test to see if it is accurate. If these options are unavailable to you, you will need to make a new ¼" guide with masking tape.

To create a new sewing guide, raise the presser foot. Then raise the unthreaded needle to its highest position. Cut out a 2" x 6" piece of ¼" graph paper. Be sure to cut accurately on the grid lines. Put the piece of graph paper under the presser foot area and lower the needle into the graph paper just barely to the right of the first ¼" grid line, on the right edge of the paper. The needle is put down to the right of the ¼" line so that it is included in the dimension of the seam allowance. Otherwise, the stitching would decrease the size of the finished area by a needle's width on each seam.

Adjust the paper so it is running straight forward from the needle and is not angled to either the left or right. Lower the presser foot to hold the paper in place. Use a piece of tape to hold the left edge of the paper so it doesn't slip.

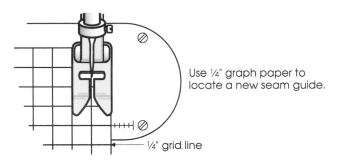

Use ¼" graph paper to locate a new seam guide.

¼" grid line

Stick a piece of masking tape on the sewing machine along the right edge of the graph paper as shown in the diagram. Make sure it is in front and out of the way of the feed dog. Make another strip test for this new guide. If it is not accurate, adjust it until you can sew an accurate strip test several times in a row. When you are satisfied that it is accurate, build up the guide with several layers of tape to create a ridge along which to guide the edge of the fabric. A piece of adhesive-backed moleskin from the drugstore also makes a good fabric guide.

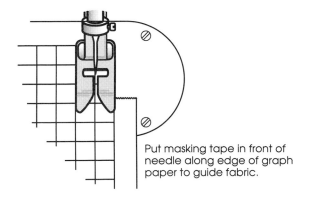

Put masking tape in front of needle along edge of graph paper to guide fabric.

Basic Stitching

To stitch rotary-cut pieces together, place them right sides together with raw edges aligned. Nubbing the corners of triangles (pages 10–11) makes it easier to align edges precisely.

Machine stitching is usually done from raw edge to raw edge, except in a few cases with special seams, when it is important to leave the seam allowances free. Backstitching is unnecessary because all stitching is usually crossed by another seam. Even the outermost border seams are secured by the stitching used to attach the binding.

Matching Seam Intersections

The easiest way to tightly match intersecting seams is to press the seam allowances in opposite directions as discussed on page 12. In this way, a ridge is formed by each of the seam allowances, and these ridges can be pushed tightly against each other. This is called butting the seams.

Sewing Partial Seams

Sometimes it is necessary to leave part of a seam unsewn. Usually, this is a situation where a block is built in a circular fashion around a central piece as shown in the block below.

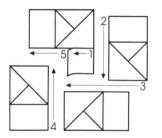

To avoid complicated piecing situations, sew the first seam partially, allowing the second seam and each subsequent seam to be sewn in place completely. The diagram shows that with the first seam only half sewn, it is easy to sew the last seam. Then it is a simple matter to finish the first seam. Backstitching is unnecessary when you overlap your beginning stitches with the last bit of stitching.

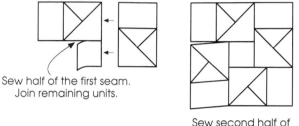

Sew half of the first seam.
Join remaining units.

Sew second half of
first seam to finish block.

Resizing Patchwork Units and Blocks

As you stitch, it's a good idea to check the dimensions of the units you have just sewn to make sure they are the correct size. Interior pieces should be the intended finished size, while outer pieces should still have ¼"-wide seam allowances on the outer edges.

Generally, any piece too small should be discarded and replaced. Sometimes, if units are too large, you can trim them down to size, using interior seams as guidelines.

How to Use This Book

The remainder of this book is organized into four pattern and skill sections. Each includes information on the cutting and piecing techniques required to make the quilts in that section.

Section One—Straight-Grain Strip Piecing
Section Two—Bias Strip Piecing
Section Three—Striped Squares and Triangles
Section Four—Curves and Diamonds

The sections build on each other progressively. For example, Section Two patterns require techniques presented in the general information and Section One, along with the techniques introduced in Section Two. Section Two does not contain any skills presented in Sections Three and Four. Also, the quilts within each section are ordered from the simpler to the more complex designs. Each section begins with a small, easy-to-make warm-up project.

FABRIC REQUIREMENTS

I try hard to reduce waste in my patterns. Cutting requirements for each fabric are listed in the most efficient order possible. Generally, I direct you to cut larger pieces that produce leftover fabric first, then cut smaller pieces from the leftovers. For example, if the first cut is a 12" x 28" piece, and ten 2½" squares are also needed from this fabric, I list the squares second so that they can be cut from the remaining 12" x 14" piece. Sometimes, instructions direct you to reserve a particular leftover piece for use later.

Even though I try to be efficient, I figure fabric requirements to give you some elbow room for errors. I know I make them. In fact, it's not a bad idea to have a little extra of each fabric on hand whenever you make a quilt, just in case you need it! Besides a major cutting blooper, there are a number of freak things that can happen, including fabric flaws, unexpected shrinkage, or a last-minute modification. You may decide to add an extra border, bind your quilt with one of the other fabrics, or change the placement of the fabrics.

All fabric and cutting requirements are based on 44"-wide fabric that shrinks to no less than 42" after washing. If your fabric measures less than 42", you will need to purchase more; how much more will vary from pattern to pattern. That's another good reason to have a little extra of each fabric. You can always add the excess to your fabric collection for future projects.

BORDER TREATMENT

In some of the patterns, you'll notice that squares cut from the border fabric are used at the corners of the borders instead of using one long border strip. This uses fabric more efficiently.

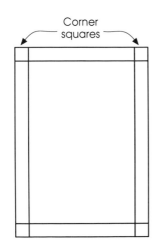

If a border measurement comes close to the 42" that you can cut across the fabric width, I prefer to piece a border strip with corner squares cut from fabric leftovers rather than to cut more border strips, which can often result in a lot of waste. If one border in a quilt calls for corner squares, then I use corner squares on all borders in that quilt for the sake of consistency. If you wish to change this approach when working with the patterns, plan ahead and buy extra fabric for the borders.

BACKING

Another way to be both frugal and creative at the same time is to piece the quilt backings. Instead of buying backing yardage that is twice the length of the quilt so that it can be pieced to fit, use the backing to showcase the fabrics left over from making the blocks. Some of my friends have creatively incorporated everything into the backing (including their mistakes, leftover strip units, and waste pieces). Even a few simple squares and triangles can add interest to a backing. Plain or fancy, pieced backings are a wonderful idea. The patterns in this book include fabric requirements for complete whole-cloth backings, pieced as needed in the standard way, but I urge you to try some simple pieced backings. See the Gallery on pages 17–32 for photos of some creatively pieced backings.

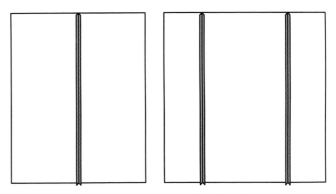

Two ways to piece standard backings.

IN SUMMARY

Please review all of the techniques in this book before starting to make one of the quilts. If you prefer a different way of doing something, you should be aware of the techniques used so that you can make any changes to accommodate your preferences before it is too late. I hope you enjoy my patterns and learn some new skills to add to your personal quiltmaking repertoire.

Gallery

◄ ***Warm-up Project***
Kansas Winds by Donna Thomas, 1993, Lansing, Kansas, 36" x 44". The intricacy of windmills within windmills belies the simple construction of this quilt. Quilted by Ann Woodward.

Cross-Eyed Puss by Donna ►
Thomas, 1993, Lansing, Kansas, 61¼" x 72⅝". This is a grown-up version of one of Donna's miniature quilts from her book Small Talk. *The combination of two blocks to create an overall design pulls the eye in a number of directions.*

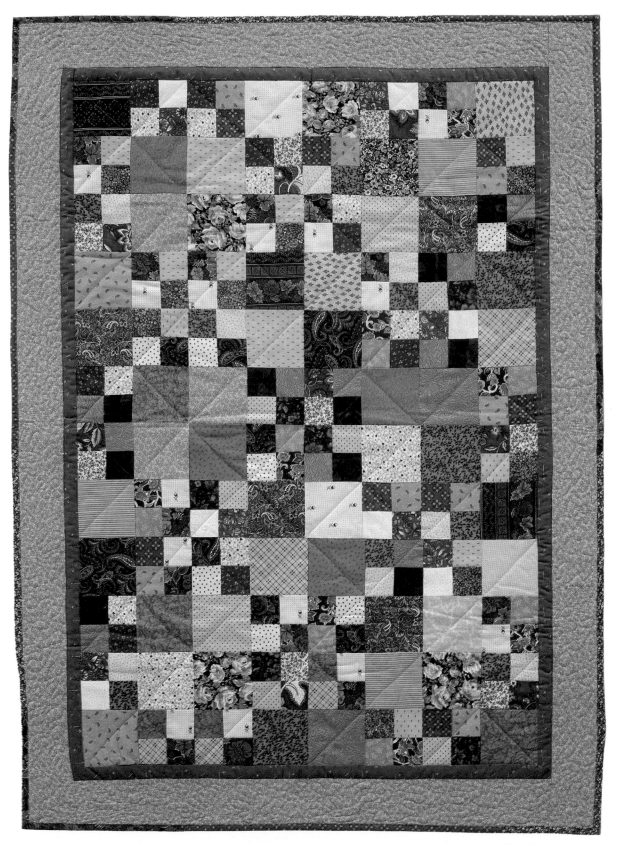

Checkerboard Chain by Donna Nagle, Fort Leavenworth, Kansas, 44" x 60". This comfy-looking scrap quilt is sure to warm the heart of some lucky veteran. Made completely from scraps, it is one of many Checkerboard Chain quilts being made by the Leavenworth Piecemakers for donation to veterans at the local VA hospital.

◀ *Checkerboard Chain by Donna Thomas, 1992, Dorf-Guell, Germany, 44" x 60". Many fabrics from one color family make this quilt sparkle. Notice the interplay of light and dark with the smaller chain overlaid on the checkerboard background. Quilted by Ann Woodward.*

Stuff of Heaven and Earth by Kari Lane, Lansing, Kansas, 44" x 60". A completely different use of fabrics results in a dynamic contemporary version of the Checkerboard Chain pattern.

▼

Stuff of Heaven and Earth by Kari Lane, Lansing, Kansas, 44" x 60". The back of the quilt is the perfect venue to show off the batik print used on the front.

▼

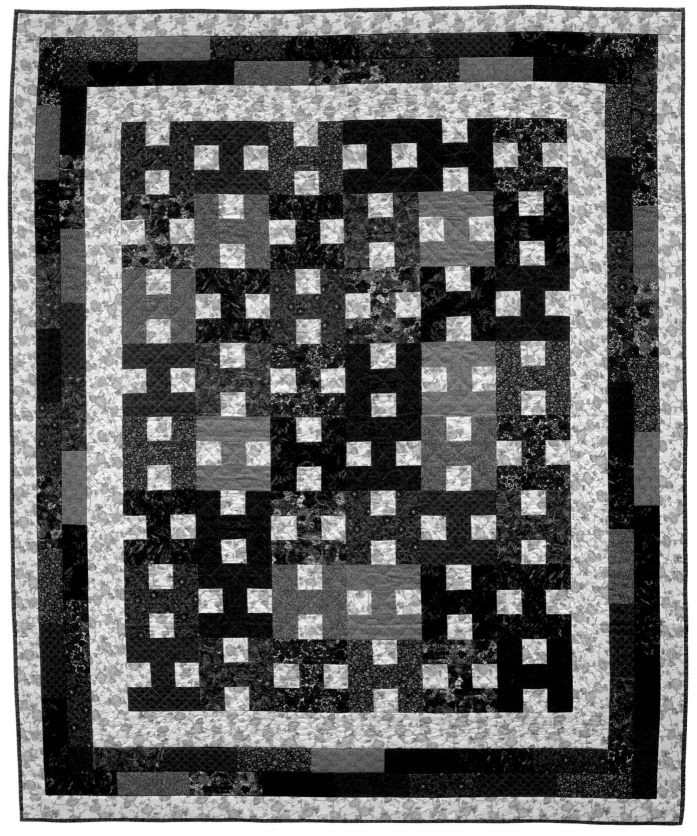

Four H by Donna Thomas, 1993, Lansing, Kansas, 54" x 66". The rich greens and brick reds bring this old-time pattern to life, while the double pieced border finishes the quilt nicely. Quilted by Ann Woodward.

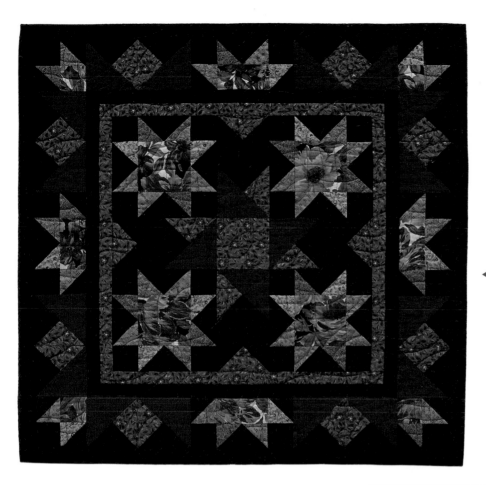

◀ ***Warm-up Project***
*Susan's Southern Star by
Donna Thomas, 1993,
Lansing, Kansas, 34" x 34".
Using a variety of gold prints
makes the stars in this small
quilt dance and twinkle. It is
machine quilted in copper
metallic thread with large
cables that weave across the
diagonal of the quilt.
Quilted by Kari Lane.*

Birds in the Air by Donna Thomas, 1992, ▶
*Dorf-Guell, Germany, 25½" x 34". Donna started
to make this little quilt with a blue/tan color
theme in mind, but she followed it loosely,
including blacks, teals, and yellows too.
Quilted by Ann Woodward.*

Birds in the Air by Donna Thomas, 1993, Lansing, Kansas, 51" x 59½". Although the quilt was assembled in 1993, the blocks have been accumulating over a number of years. Fabric exchanges, treasured scraps, specialty or novelty fabrics, unusual color combinations—all can be used successfully in a scrap quilt like this one. Quilted by Kari Lane.

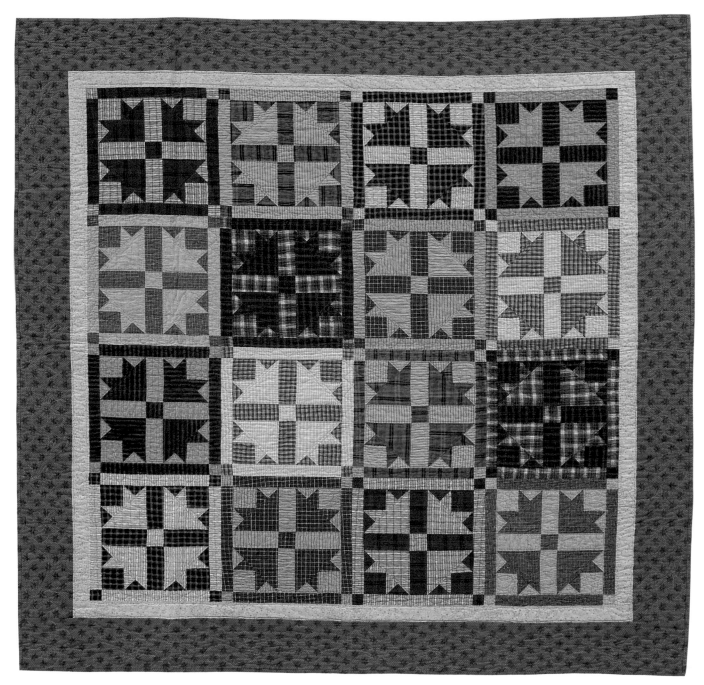

Turkey Tracks by Donna Thomas, 1992, Lansing, Kansas, 58" x 58". Fat-quarter collections of homespuns inspired this wonderfully antique-looking quilt. Cotton batting and a lot of beautiful hand quilting make this quilt irresistible to snuggle under for a winter nap. Quilted by Aline Duerr and Norma Jean Rohman.

Mosaic Sparkler by Donna Thomas, 1992, Lansing, Kansas, 48" x 64". Mosaic is a traditional pattern that takes on new life when the blocks are set together side by side. Rather than sew solid strips for the borders of this multi-fabric quilt, Donna used squares of the different fabrics left over from the blocks to make pieced borders for even more visual interest. Leftover fabric strips were even used to piece the binding. Quilted by Roxanne Carter.

Section
THREE
Striped Squares and Triangles

Warm-up Project
Double Star by Donna Thomas, 1992, Lansing, Kansas, 45" x 55". Hope of Hartford, a traditional block, was the basis for this design. With a few line changes here and there, a wonderful overall design appears. Striped squares make this quilt wonderfully easy to assemble. Quilted by Kari Lane.

Shifting Winds by Donna Thomas, 1993, Lansing, Kansas, 56" x 56". The traditional Dutch Windmill block is reminiscent of a child's carnival pinwheel. Shifting the spin on the blocks gave the quilt its name. The warm rusty red and cool blue green tones complement each other well. Quilted by Maureen McGee.

Four Patch Ripple by M. Deborah Rose, 1993, Fort Leavenworth, Kansas, 56" x 64". Although the blocks are set straight, there is a definite diagonal feel to the design of this cheerful Christmas quilt. The green striped triangles ripple on the diagonal between chains of red squares. The two-tone pieced border contains it all.

Spools by Donna Thomas, 1993, Lansing, Kansas, 56" x 64". This old favorite adapts beautifully to new rotary techniques. Lots of fabrics from two color families keep the quilt lively, while smaller spools dance around the inner pieced border. Quilted by Ann Woodward.

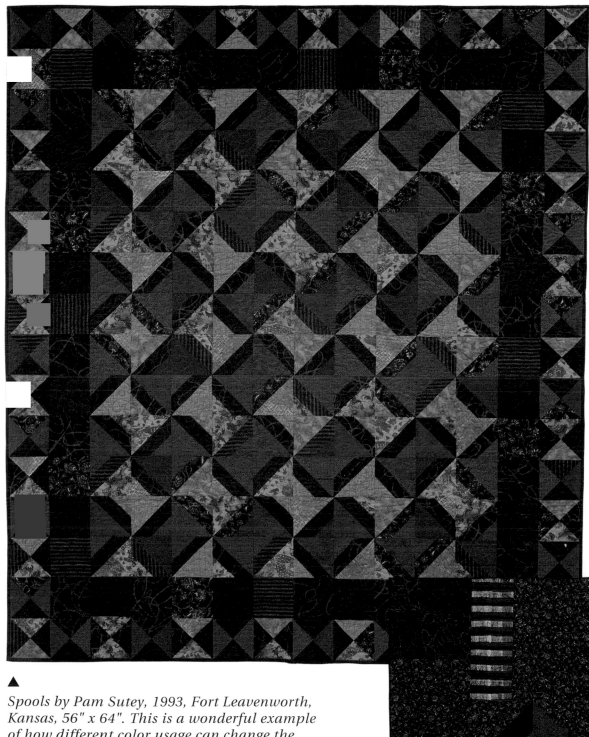

▲

Spools by Pam Sutey, 1993, Fort Leavenworth, Kansas, 56" x 64". This is a wonderful example of how different color usage can change the entire look of the same pattern. The purple and teal spools tend to stand out and recede, depending on how you look at the quilt.

Spools by Pam Sutey, 1993, Fort Leavenworth, Kansas, 56" x 64". The spool motif was successfully brought to the back of this quilt while making good use of leftover fabric pieces. ▶

◀ ***Warm-up Project***
Sunny Day in the Garden by Tamie Renbarger, 1993, Fort Leavenworth, Kansas, 35⅛" x 46⅜". Summer has arrived and the garden is bright and sunny. Straight seams were used to make the square buds in these flowers.

Rainy Day in the Garden by Donna Thomas, 1992, Lansing, Kansas, 35⅛" x 46⅜". The gray overtones are reminiscent of a cool and rainy spring day in the garden. The rounded buds are sewn with curved seams. Quilted by Aline Duerr and Norma Jean Rohman. ▶

Starbloom by Roxanne Carter, 1993, Mukilteo, Washington, 43" x 43". The elegance of this design is beautifully reflected in the fabrics chosen. On the other hand, solids would work equally well in the striped diamonds to lend a more contemporary feel to this quilt.

▲
Glory of the Season by M. Deborah Rose, 1993, Fort Leavenworth, Kansas, 41" x 47". What could be more glorious than the true colors of autumn? Fall leaves line the forest floor in this quilted tribute to color.

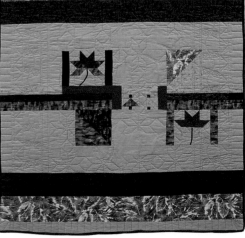

Glory of the Season by M. Deborah Rose, 1993, Fort Leavenworth, Kansas, 41" x 47". Surprise! A stray leaf or two found their way to the back of this quilt. ▶

Straight-Grain Strip Piecing

Straight-grain strip piecing is simple to illustrate with the humble Ninepatch block. Using traditional methods, you cut individual squares and then sew them together one-by-one to assemble this simple block. If you break the Ninepatch block into its three rows, you can see that rows 1 and 3 are identical and row 2 is composed of the same shapes and colors but in a different arrangement.

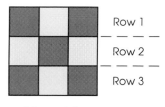

Ninepatch

To speed up the assembly process, you can cut straight-grain strips of fabric and sew them together side by side, then cut them into segments that look like the rows in the Ninepatch block. Then, it is a simple matter to sew the segments together to complete the block.

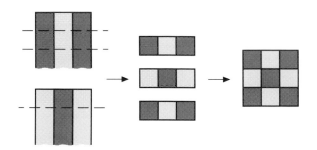

ASSEMBLING STRAIGHT-GRAIN STRIP UNITS

Straight-grain strip units are made of two or more straight-grain strips sewn together, side by side.

1. Cut strips perpendicular to the selvage, across the fabric width, cutting them the width given in the quilt directions you are following.
2. Remove selvages from all strips before using them in a strip unit of any kind.
3. Cut all full-length (42") strips in half to 21" before working with them unless instructed otherwise. Full-length strip units tend to curve

after sewing, making them difficult to cut accurately into the required units. Half-length strip units are less likely to curve and are easier to handle. All patterns in this book use half-length strip units.

4. Press seams as you go. It's easier. Remember to press seams from the right side.

CUTTING SEGMENTS

1. Make a clean cut along the short edge of the strip unit. This is your cutting edge. It is important to make all cuts at right angles to the strip-unit seams, or you will have cockeyed squares and rectangles.

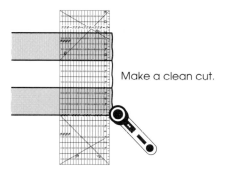

Make a clean cut.

2. Turn the strip unit around as shown and position the ruler the required distance from the cutting edge for the segments. Be sure to line up the horizontal ruler lines on the strip seams so you make a right-angle cut.

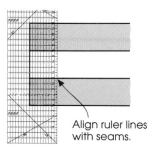

Align ruler lines with seams.

3. If, at any time, the short edge and interior seams no longer form a right angle, make a new, clean cut on the short edge. It is normal to make this adjustment periodically due to the minuscule amount of ruler slippage that occurs with each cut. The more carefully you cut, the less frequently you'll have to trim the raw edge.

Warm-up
PROJECT
Kansas Winds

Finished Size: 36" x 44"

Finished Block Size: 8"

Color photo on page 17

Practice the basics of straight-grain strip piecing with this lively little quilt. There are three simple strip units to construct, and the blocks fit together easily.

The quilt requires dark and light fabrics from two color families. The border fabric will be the most predominate, so you may want to choose it first.

Materials: 44"-wide fabric

½ yd. dark green

½ yd. light green

¾ yd. cranberry red

½ yd. pink

⅜ yd. for binding

1½ yds. for backing

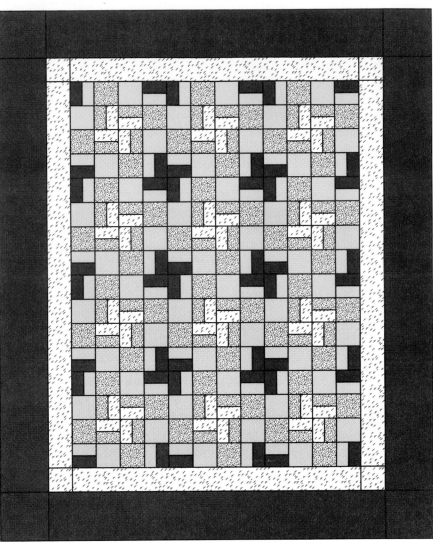

Color Key

Dark green

Light green

Cranberry red

Pink

Kansas Winds
Make 12.

Cutting: All measurements include ¼"-wide seam allowances.

From the dark green, cut:
3 strips, each 2½" x 42"; crosscut into:
    6 strips, each 2½" x 21", for Strip Unit I;

3 strips, each 1½" x 42"; crosscut into:
    6 strips, each 1½" x 21", for Strip Unit II.

From the light green, cut:
3 strips, each 1½" x 42"; crosscut into:
    6 strips, each 1½" x 21", for Strip Unit II;

4 strips, each 2½" x 42", for the inner border.

From the cranberry red, cut:
3 strips, each 1½" x 42"; crosscut into:
    6 strips, each 1½" x 21", for Strip Unit III;

4 strips, each 4½" x 42", for the outer border.

From the pink, cut:
3 strips, each 2½" x 42"; crosscut into:
   6 strips, each 2½" x 21", for Strip Unit I;

3 strips, each 1½" x 42"; crosscut into:
   6 strips, each 1½" x 21", for Strip Unit III.

From the fabric for binding, cut:
4 strips, each 2" x 42".

Piecing the Blocks
Press seam allowances in the direction of the arrows unless otherwise instructed.

1. Assemble strip units as shown below. Cut a total of 48 segments, each 2½" wide, from each of Strip Units I, II, and III.

Strip Unit I: 2½" x 21" dark green and pink strips.

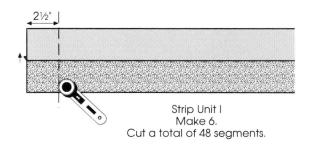

Strip Unit I
Make 6.
Cut a total of 48 segments.

Strip Unit II: 1½" x 21" dark green and light green strips.

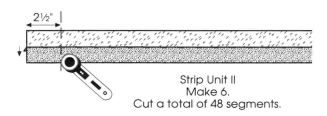

Strip Unit II
Make 6.
Cut a total of 48 segments.

Strip Unit III: 1½" x 21" cranberry red and pink strips.

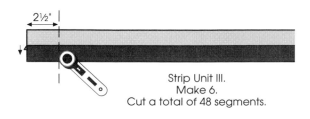

Strip Unit III.
Make 6.
Cut a total of 48 segments.

2. Sew Strip Unit II segments together as shown.

Make 24.

3. Sew the resulting units into 12 pairs as shown. Press the center seam in opposite directions as indicated by the arrows. See "Pressing" on page 12, option 1.

Make 12.

4. Sew a Strip Unit I segment to each side of the unit made in step 3.

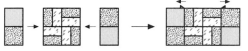

Make 12.

5. Sew a Strip Unit III segment to each side of the remaining Strip Unit I segments.

Make 24.

6. Sew the resulting units to each side of the units made in step 4 to complete the blocks.

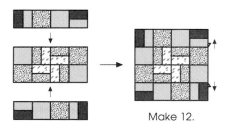

Make 12.

Assembling and Finishing the Quilt Top

1. Arrange the blocks in rows, orienting the seams of the completed blocks as shown. Stitch. Press the seams in opposite directions from row to row.

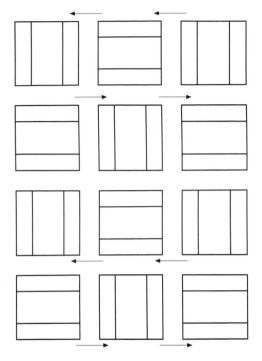

2. Join the rows to complete the quilt top.
3. Refer to the directions on page 94 for measuring, cutting, and attaching borders with corner squares. Trim 2 light green 2½" x 42" inner border strips to match the center length measurement of the quilt top for the side borders. Trim the other 2 light green inner border strips to match the center width measurement of the quilt top for top and bottom borders. Sew side borders to the quilt top; press seams toward the border.
4. Cut 4 corner squares, each 2½" x 2½", from the leftover light green strips, and sew a square to each end of the top and bottom border strips; press seams toward the border strip. Sew the border strips to the top and bottom of the quilt top; press seams toward the border.
5. Measure, trim, and sew the 4½" cranberry red outer border strips to the quilt top as described for the inner border. Cut 4 corner squares, each 4½" x 4½" from leftover cranberry red strips.
6. Layer the completed quilt top with batting and backing; baste.
7. Quilt as desired.
8. Bind the edges, following the directions on pages 95–96.

Four H

Finished Size: 54" x 66"

Finished Block Size: 6"

Color photo on page 20

Four H is an old-time pattern that is well suited to straight-grain strip piecing with many fabrics. Select a number of fabrics from two different color families. Use a partial seam to attach the second pieced border.

Materials: 44"-wide fabric

¼ yd. each of 6 green prints

¼ yd. each of 6 brick red prints

1⅝ yds. coordinating light print

½ yd. for binding

4 yds. for backing

Color Key

Greens

Brick reds

Light

Four H
Make 24 green.
Make 24 brick red.

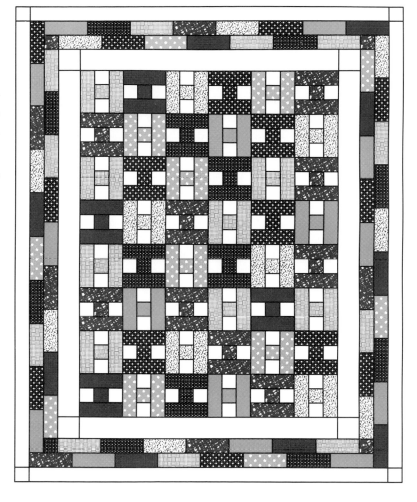

Cutting: All measurements include ¼"-wide seam allowances.

From each of the 6 green prints, cut:
3 strips, each 2½" x 42"; crosscut into:
    14 bars, each 2½" x 6½", for the blocks and pieced borders;
    1 strip, 2½" x 12", for the strip unit.

From each of the 6 brick red prints, cut:
3 strips, each 2½" x 42"; crosscut into:
    14 bars, each 2½" x 6½", for the blocks and pieced borders;
    1 strip, 2½" x 12", for the strip unit.

From each of 4 brick red prints, cut:
1 square, 2½" x 2½", for inner pieced border.

From the coordinating light print, cut:
8 strips, each 2½" x 42"; crosscut into:
    24 strips, each 2½" x 12", for strip units;

5 strips, each 3½" x 42", for inner border;

6 strips, each 2½" x 42", for outer border.

From the fabric for binding, cut:
6 strips, each 2" x 42".

Piecing the Blocks

Press seam allowances in the direction of the arrows unless otherwise instructed.

1. Using the 2½" x 12" strips, sew a light-print strip to each side of each green and each brick red strip.
2. Cut a total of 48 segments, each 2½" wide, from the strip units. Separate the segments into groups of matching brick red or green prints.

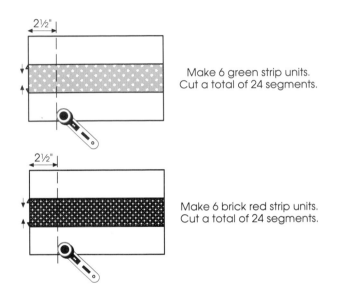

Make 6 green strip units.
Cut a total of 24 segments.

Make 6 brick red strip units.
Cut a total of 24 segments.

3. Sew a matching green or brick red 2½" x 6½" bar to each side of each segment cut in step 2 to complete the blocks.

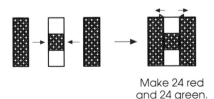

Make 24 red
and 24 green.

Assembling and Finishing the Quilt Top

1. Arrange the Four H blocks in rows, alternating colors and directions as shown in the quilt plan on page 37. Stitch. Press block seams in opposite directions from row to row. Join the rows to complete the quilt top.

2. Cut 1 light-print 3½" x 42" inner border strip in half crosswise. Sew a half strip to one end of 2 of the 42"-long strips.
3. Refer to the directions on page 94 for measuring, cutting, and attaching borders with corner squares. Trim the 2 inner border strips from step 2 to match the center length measurement of the quilt top for side borders. Trim the remaining 2 border strips to match the center width measurement of the quilt top for top and bottom borders. Sew side borders to quilt top. Press seams toward the border.
4. Cut 4 corner squares, each 3½" x 3½", from leftover inner border strips, and sew a square to each end of the top and bottom border strips; press seams toward the border strips. Sew the border strips with corner squares to the top and bottom of the quilt top; press seams toward the border.
5. Using 5 green and 4 brick red 2½" x 6½" bars and alternating the colors, make 2 inner border strips for the sides. Press seams to one side. Using 4 green and 3 brick red 2½" x 6½" bars and alternating the colors, make 2 inner border strips for the top and bottom of the quilt. Press seams to one side. Sew a 2½" brick red square to each end of the top and bottom border strips. Press seams toward the center.

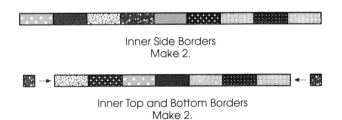

Inner Side Borders
Make 2.

Inner Top and Bottom Borders
Make 2.

6. Before attaching the pieced border, measure the quilt top. It should measure 42½" x 54½". If it is larger or smaller, the pieced border will not fit. You can ease minor differences by adjusting the seams in the pieced border, making a few of them slightly wider or narrower so the border strip will fit the quilt top.
7. Sew the pieced side border strips to the sides of the quilt top first; press seams toward the pieced border. Add the top and bottom inner pieced border strips to the quilt top; press seams toward the border.

8. Using 5 green and 5 red 2½" x 6½" bars and alternating the colors, make 2 middle side border strips. Using 4 green and 4 red bars, make 2 middle top and bottom border strips. Press seams to one side.

Middle Side Borders
Make 2.

Middle Top and Bottom Borders
Make 2.

Note: Measure the quilt top. It should measure 46½" x 58½". If not, adjust the border strips as described in step 6 for the first pieced border.

9. Sew the second pieced border to the quilt one side at a time, in a counterclockwise direction. Sew the first strip to the right side of the quilt. Stop stitching 6" from the bottom end. Remove from the machine and press the seam toward the outer border.

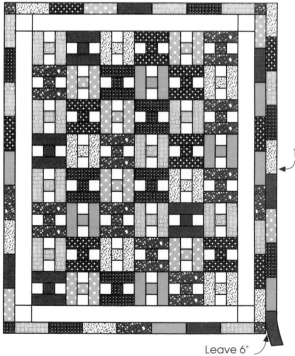

1

Leave 6"
unstitched.

10. Sew the remaining borders to the quilt in numerical order as shown. Press seams toward the outer border. After sewing the bottom border strip to the quilt, sew the remaining 6" of the first strip to complete the border.

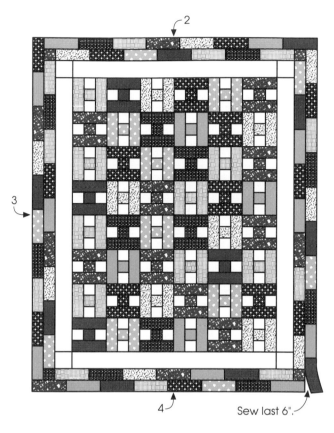

2

3

4

Sew last 6".

11. Cut 2 light-print 2½" x 42" outer border strips in half crosswise. Sew a half strip to one end of the 4 remaining 42"-long strips. Press seams to one side.

12. Measure, trim, and sew the outer border strips to the quilt top as described for the inner border. Cut 4 corner squares, each 2½" x 2½", from leftover outer border strips

13. Layer the completed quilt top with batting and backing; baste.

14. Quilt as desired.

15. Bind the edges, following the directions on pages 95–96.

Checkerboard Chain

Finished Size: 44" x 60"

Block A Finished Size: 8"

Block B Finished Size: 8"

Color photos on pages 18–19

This quilt, made with many different red prints, is a beautiful example of dark and light contrast. You can also use a range of colors in a scrappy version, which offers you a terrific opportunity to use up leftover strips from other projects.

Materials: 44"-wide fabric

⅜ yd. each of 6 medium-dark prints **OR** an 18" x 22" fat quarter of each

¼ yd. each of 6 light prints **OR** a 12" x 21" piece of each

⅜ yd. dark print for inner border

⅝ yd. light print for middle border

½ yd. for binding

3½ yds. for backing

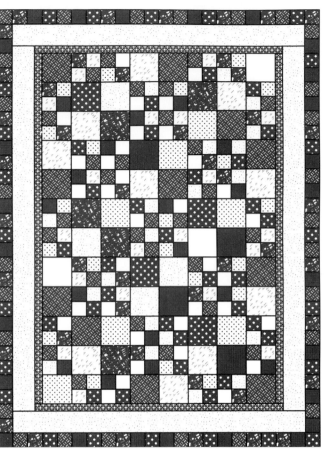

Color Key

Medium-darks

Lights

Dark

Block A
Make 12.

Block B
Make 12.

Cutting: All measurements include ¼"-wide seam allowances.

From each of the 6 medium-dark prints, cut:
1 strip, 2½" x 42"; crosscut into:
    2 strips, each 2½" x 21", for strip units;

1 strip, 4½" x 42"; crosscut into:
    4 squares, each 4½" x 4½", for blocks;
    1 square, 2½" x 2½", for outer pieced border;

1 strip, 2½" x 42"; crosscut into:
    16 squares, each 2½" x 2½", for outer pieced border.

From each of the 6 light prints, cut:
1 strip, 2½" x 42"; crosscut into:
    2 strips, each 2½" x 21", for strip units;

1 strip, 4½" x 42"; crosscut into:
    4 squares, each 4½" x 4½", for blocks.

From the dark print for inner border, cut:
5 strips, each 1½" x 42".

From the light print for middle border, cut:
5 strips, each 3½" x 42".

From the fabric for binding, cut:
6 strips, each 2" x 42".

Piecing the Blocks

Press seam allowances in the direction of the arrows unless otherwise instructed.

1. Using the 2½" x 21" strips, sew 1 dark and 1 light strip together. Cut a total of 96 segments, each 2½" wide, from the strip units.

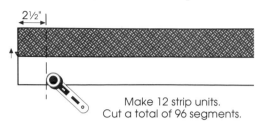

Make 12 strip units.
Cut a total of 96 segments.

2. Sew the segments into a four-patch unit as shown. Side A is the side on which the final seam is pressed toward the light square.

Side A

Make 48.

Note: Feed the pairs into the machine with the dark square of the top segment first.

3. Sew a four-patch unit to a 4½" light-print square as shown. Position Side A of the four-patch unit toward the large square. This is very imporant for assembly. In the same manner, sew a four-patch unit to a 4½" dark-print square.

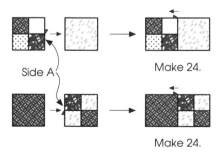

Side A

Make 24.

Make 24.

4. Pair the four-patch/dark-square units to make 12 Block A. Pair the four-patch/light square units to make 12 Block B. Be careful to position the block halves properly before sewing. Stitch and press.

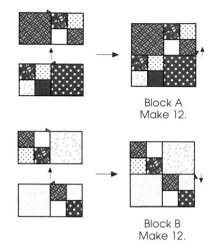

Block A
Make 12.

Block B
Make 12.

Assembling and Finishing the Quilt Top

1. Arrange 12 Block A and 12 Block B as shown below. Position each of the blocks with Block A center seams facing up and Block B center seams facing down. Stitch. Press seams in opposite directions from row to row.

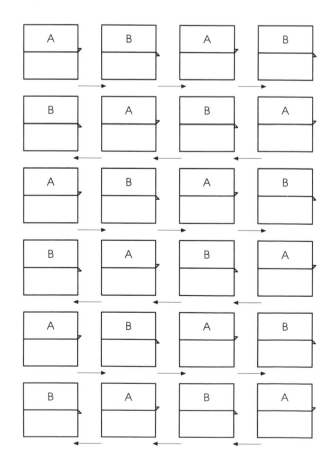

2. Sew the rows together and press.
3. Cut 1 dark 1½" x 42" inner border strip in half crosswise. Sew a half strip to one end of 2 of the 42"-long strips to make 2 pieced side border strips.
4. Refer to the directions on page 94 for measuring, cutting, and attaching borders with straight-cut corners. Trim the 2 border strips from step 3 to match the center length measurement of the quilt top and sew to the sides; press seams toward the border.
5. Trim the 2 remaining inner border strips to match the center width measurement of the quilt top and sew to the top and bottom; press seams toward the border.
6. Cut 1 light-print 3½" x 42" middle border strips in half crosswise. Sew a half strip to one end of 2 of the 42"-long strips to make 2 pieced side borders. Measure, trim, and sew the middle border strips to the quilt top as described for the inner border. Press seams toward the middle border.
7. Placing the various prints randomly, sew together 28 medium-dark 2½" squares for each outer pieced side border. Sew together 22 medium-dark squares for each pieced top and bottom border strip. Press seams to one side, except for the end squares, which should be pressed out toward the ends of the border strip.

Note: Before attaching the outer pieced border, measure the completed quilt top. It should measure 40½" x 56½". If it is larger or smaller, the pieced border will not fit. You can ease minor differences by adjusting the seams in the pieced border, making a few of them slightly wider or narrower so the border strip will fit the quilt top.

8. Sew the pieced border strips to the sides and then to the top and bottom of the quilt top. Press seams toward the middle border strips. (Pressing seams toward pieced borders is difficult.)
9. Layer the completed quilt top with batting and backing; baste.
10. Quilt as desired.
11. Bind the edges, following the directions on pages 95–96.

Cross-Eyed Puss

Finished Size: 61¼" x 72⅝"

Puss in the Corner (Block A)
Finished Block Size: 8"

Cross Block (Block B)
Finished Size: 8"

Color photo on page 17

If you enjoy miniature quilts, you may recognize this quilt as a grown-up version of one shown on the cover of my book Small Talk. This variation uses two pink prints instead of one. Select the prominent border fabric first.

Materials: 44"-wide fabric

1⅝ yds. dark blue

½ yd. medium blue

⅞ yd. light blue

¼ yd. dark red

1¼ yds. medium red

⅝ yd. medium pink

⅝ yd. light pink

½ yd. for binding

5 yds. for backing

Color Key

Dark blue   Medium red

Medium blue   Medium pink

Light blue   Light pink

Dark red

Block A
Make 20.

Block B
Make 12.

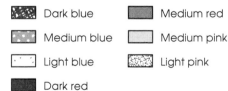

Side Setting Triangles
Make 14.

Corner Triangles
Make 4.

Cutting: All measurements include ¼"-wide seam allowances.

From the dark blue, cut:
3 strips, each 4½" x 42"; crosscut into:
    5 strips, each 4½" x 21", for Strip Unit II;

6 strips, each 6½" x 42", for outer border.

From the medium blue, cut:
5 strips, each 2½" x 42"; crosscut into:
    10 strips, each 2½" x 21", for Strip Unit I.

From the light blue, cut:
3 strips, each 4½" x 42"; crosscut into:
    5 strips, each 4½" x 21", for Strip Unit I;

5 strips, each 2½" x 42"; crosscut into:
    10 strips, each 2½" x 21", for Strip Unit II.

From the dark red, cut:
1 strip, 2½" x 42"; crosscut into:
    2 strips, each 2½" x 21", for Strip Unit IV;

1 strip, 4⅛" x 42"; crosscut into:
    4 squares, each 4⅛" x 4⅛", for side setting
      triangles;
    2 squares, each 2⅜" x 2⅜", for pieced
      corner triangles.

From the medium red, cut:
2 strips, each 3½" x 42"; crosscut into:
    4 strips, each 3½" x 21", for Strip Unit IV;

6 strips, each 2½" x 42"; crosscut into:
    5 strips, each 2½" x 21", for Strip Unit III;
    3 strips, each 2½" x 21", for Strip Unit V;
    18 bars, each 2½" x 3½", for pieced side
      setting and corner triangles;

6 strips, each 2½" x 42", for inner border.

From the medium pink, cut:
2 strips, each 5½" x 42"; crosscut into:
    9 squares, each 5½" x 5½", for pieced side
      setting and corner triangles;
    1 strip, 3½" x 21", for Strip Unit V;

1 strip, 3½" x 42"; crosscut into:
    2 strips, each 3½" x 21", for Strip Unit V.

From the light pink, cut:
5 strips, each 3½" x 42"; crosscut into:
    10 strips, each 3½" x 21", for Strip Unit III.

From the fabric for binding, cut:
8 strips, each 2" x 42".

Piecing the Blocks and Setting Triangles
Press seam allowances in the direction of the arrows unless otherwise instructed.

Block A
1. Using the medium blue 2½" x 21" strips and the light blue 4½" x 21" strips, make 5 Strip Unit I as shown. Cut a total of 40 segments, each 2½" wide, from Strip Unit I.

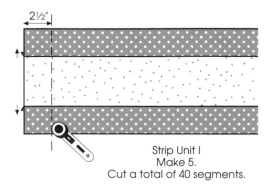

Strip Unit I
Make 5.
Cut a total of 40 segments.

2. Using the dark blue 4½" x 21" strips and the light blue 2½" x 21" strips, make 5 Strip Unit II as shown. Cut a total of 20 segments, each 4½" wide, from Strip Unit II.

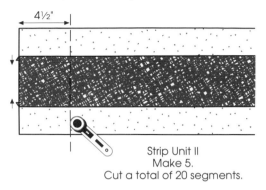

Strip Unit II
Make 5.
Cut a total of 20 segments.

3. Sew a Strip Unit I segment to each side of a Strip Unit II segment to make Block A.

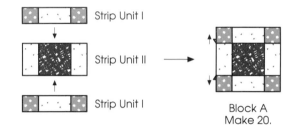

Block A
Make 20.

Block B
1. Using the light pink 3½" x 21" strips and the medium red 2½" x 21" strips, make 5 Strip Unit III as shown. Cut a total of 24 segments, each 3½" wide, from Strip Unit III.

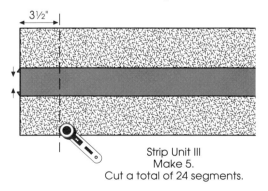

Strip Unit III
Make 5.
Cut a total of 24 segments.

2. Using the medium red 3½" x 21" strips and the dark red 2½" x 21" strips, make 2 Strip Unit IV as shown. Cut a total of 12 segments, each 2½" wide, from Strip Unit IV.

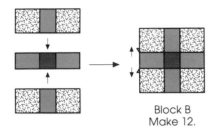

Strip Unit IV
Make 2.
Cut a total of 12 segments.

3. Sew a Strip Unit III segment to each side of a Strip Unit IV segment to make Block B.

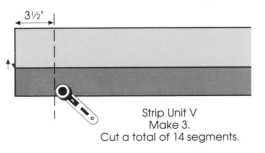

Block B
Make 12.

Side Setting Triangles

1. Using the medium pink 3½" x 21" strips and the 3 remaining medium red 2½" x 21" strips, make 3 Strip Unit V. Cut a total of 14 segments, each 3½" wide, from Strip Unit V.

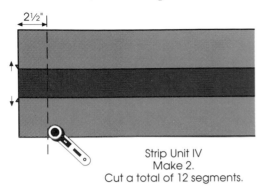

Strip Unit V
Make 3.
Cut a total of 14 segments.

2. Cut the 4 dark red 4⅛" squares twice diagonally to yield 16 quarter-square triangles. You will need 14. Sew a dark red quarter-square triangle to a medium red 2½" x 3½" bar as shown.

Make 14.

3. Sew each bar/triangle unit to a Strip Unit V segment.

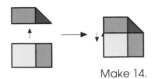

Make 14.

4. Cut 9 medium pink 5½" squares twice diagonally to yield 36 quarter-square triangles. Sew 2 triangles to each of the units made in step 4. Reserve the remaining 8 triangles for corners.

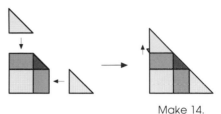

Make 14.

Corner Triangles

1. Sew a reserved medium pink quarter-square triangle from step 5 above to each side of the 4 remaining 2½" x 3½" medium red bars.

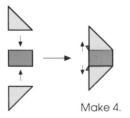

Make 4.

2. Cut the 2 dark red 2⅜" squares once diagonally to yield 4 half-square triangles. Sew a dark red half-square triangle to each of the units made in step 1 to complete the corner triangle units.

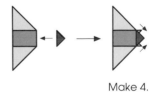

Make 4.

Assembling and Finishing the Quilt Top

1. Arrange Blocks A and B and the side setting triangles in diagonal rows as shown below. Stitch. Press seams toward Block B and the side setting triangles. Join the rows and press.

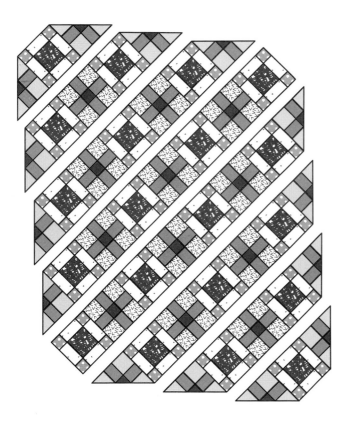

2. Center a corner triangle unit on each corner of the quilt top. Stitch. Press seams toward the outside edges.

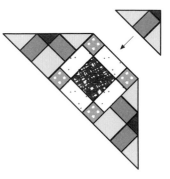

3. Cut 2 medium red 2½" x 42" inner border strips in half crosswise. Sew a half strip to one end of each of the remaining 42"-long strips.

4. Refer to the directions on page 94 for measuring, cutting, and attaching borders with straight-cut corners. Cut 2 of the inner border strips from step 3 to match the center length measurement of the quilt top and sew to the sides; press seams toward the border.

5. Cut the other 2 inner border strips to match the center width measurement of the quilt top and sew to the top and bottom; press seams toward the border.

6. Cut 2 dark blue 6½" x 42" outer border strips in half crosswise. Sew a half strip to one end of each of the remaining 42"-long strips. Measure, trim, and sew the dark blue outer border strips to the quilt top as described for the inner border.

7. Layer the completed quilt top with batting and backing; baste.

8. Quilt as desired.

9. Bind the edges, following the directions on pages 95–96.

Bias Strip Piecing

In Section Two, you will cut and use bias strips to assemble bias squares and side-by-side triangles. A bias square is composed of two right triangles joined on the long edges. This triangle combination is used extensively in both traditional and contemporary quilt patterns. In most cases, the outside edges of a bias square are cut on the straight grain (to avoid stretching) and with the square's diagonal seam on the bias.

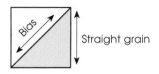

Squares cut from two straight-grain strips sewn together have bias edges.

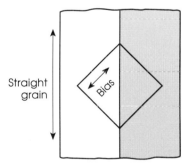

Bias strips sewn together yield bias squares with straight-grain edges.

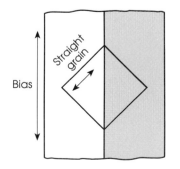

CUTTING AND SEWING
BIAS STRIP UNITS

There are 2 methods for cutting bias strips. They are both based on the premise that the diagonal of any straight-grain square is bias.

Method
ONE

Use this method to make a small number of bias squares. Cut bias strips from squares and sew strips in pairs. The size squares needed are indicated in each quilt plan that use this method.
1. With right sides together, layer two squares of the same size from contrasting fabric.
2. Cut the layered squares diagonally through the center. From either side of this center diagonal, cut all of the fabric into bias strips.

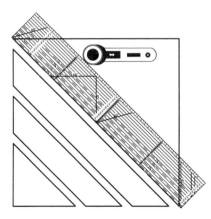

3. Pick up the bias strips in pairs and sew them as they are layered, along the long edges.

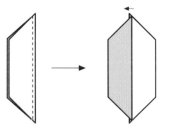

4. For maximum use of fabric, sew the bias strip pairs together into multiple bias strip units, keeping the units together according to length and the points even on one edge.

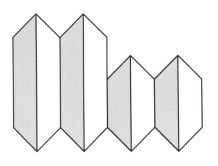

Method
TWO

To produce larger quantities of bias squares, cut bias strips from longer pieces of fabric. Generally, these pieces are cut selvage to selvage from fabric yardage; for example, a 12" x 42" piece of fabric. Sometimes a full 42" piece is not needed and less will be indicated in the pattern, such as a 12" x 34" piece.

1. Layer two rectangles of fabric, each cut the same size, placing them both face up or both face down. The selvages will be on the left and right. Once positioned, remove the selvages.

2. Measure along the bottom edge of the fabrics, out from the left corner to a point equal to the height of the pieces. Make a mark at this point. Cut diagonally from the mark on the lower edge to the upper left corner. Use the 45° angle of your ruler on the selvage edge.

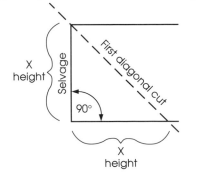

3. Cut bias strips parallel to the cut edge across the width of the fabric. Note the different types of cut strips identified in the diagram.

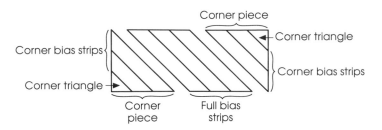

Note: Sometimes the last full bias strip on the right comes up short at the lower right corner. As long as the point is clipped less than 1"–1½", this "clipped" bias strip is still usable in the bias strip unit.

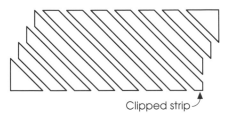

Clipped strip

4. Separate the layers of strips and organize them into a bias strip unit by length as shown. Lay out the full-size strips first, alternating prints. Then add corner bias strips to each end, again being sure to alternate prints. If you have cut several different lengths of corner bias strips, add the larger ones first.

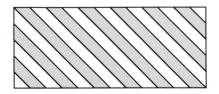

It is important to do two things when sewing a Method Two multiple bias strip unit:
1. Always sew from the top of the strip unit to the bottom so that the top edge of the strip unit is aligned. This makes cutting bias squares from the unit easier.

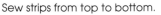
Sew strips from top to bottom.

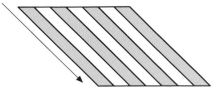

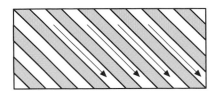

2. Offset the strips. Begin stitching at the V, where the angled edges of the two strips intersect. This yields a strip unit that is even along the top edge and down one side, making it easier to cut bias squares.

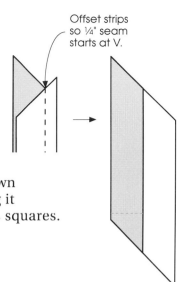

Offset strips so ¼" seam starts at V.

DETERMINING BIAS STRIP WIDTH

The width you cut bias strips is the same whether you are working with Method One or Method Two. The desired bias strip width is figured mathematically by multiplying the finished size of the desired bias square by .71. Then round up the measurement to the nearest ⅛" and add ⅝" to this figure. Cut strips this width for single pairs of bias strips.

For multiple bias strip units, add ⅞" to this figure. If you would like more "elbow room" in your strip width, you may add ¾" for single bias strip units and 1" for multiple bias strip units.

PRESSING BIAS STRIPS

Refer to the general guidelines for pressing on pages 12–13 and follow the suggestions below.

• It is easier to press bias strip seams one at a time, as you sew.

• Be careful when handling bias strips. Remember that bias edges stretch and distort easily.

• Use a light touch and press bias strips in the direction of the straight of grain.

CUTTING BIAS SQUARES

Use a Bias Square ruler to cut bias squares from the sewn and pressed strip units. The Bias Square ruler has a diagonal line and ⅛" markings that meet in the center to form squares at ⅛" increments.

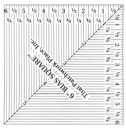

To cut bias squares from Method One bias strip units:

1. Begin at the lower end of the bias strip unit and position the diagonal line of the Bias Square ruler on the seam. The numbers on the ruler should be at the top.

2. To cut the first bias square from the lower points, make sure the desired dimensions are just inside the raw edges at the bottom of the strip unit. Cut the top two edges of the bias square from raw edge to raw edge.

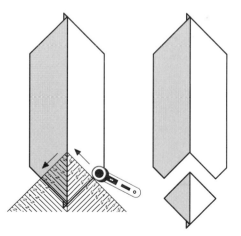

3. Turn the bias square and trim the remaining two raw edges to the proper size by aligning the markings on the Bias Square ruler with the clean-cut edges.

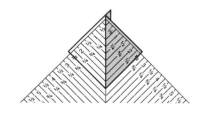

4. Use the same procedure to cut bias squares from multiple bias strip units. Begin cutting from the lowest point. Move systematically from either left to right or right to left.

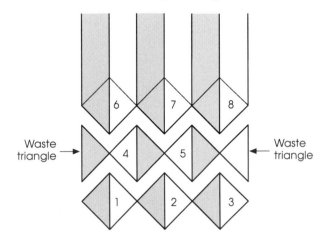

Waste triangle →
← Waste triangle

5. There will be leftover triangles at the edges of the strips. If you do not need to use these triangles, reduce the number of triangles by sewing single pairs of bias strips into multiple bias strip units. Fewer outside strip edges result in fewer waste triangles.

To cut bias squares from Method Two bias strip units:

1. Position the strip unit with the even edge toward you.
2. Cut bias squares, beginning at the bottom even edge and following the same basic procedures as for Method One. *There may be slivers of fabric between each bias square.*

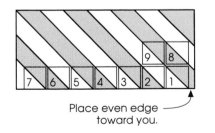

Place even edge toward you.

CUTTING BIAS SQUARES
INTO SIDE-BY-SIDES

Side-by-sides are two quarter-square triangles sewn together along the short sides to form a larger triangle. Instead of sewing single triangles together, cut presewn side-by-sides from bias squares by cutting a bias square in half diagonally to yield two mirror-image side-by-sides.

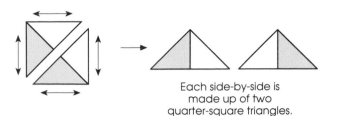

Each side-by-side is made up of two quarter-square triangles.

MAKING SIDE-BY-SIDE
BIAS STRIP UNITS

1. For either Method One or Method Two bias strip units, multiply the finished size of the outer edge of a side-by-side by .71.

Finished size

Round up to nearest ⅛" increment. Add ⅞" to this figure and cut bias strips this width for single bias strip units. For multiple bias strip units, add 1⅛" to this figure. If you'd like a little more "elbow room" with your strip widths, you may add 1" for single bias strip units and 1¼" for multiple bias strip units.

Example:

2" (finished size) x .71 = 1.42 (Round up to 1½".)

Single bias strip unit = 1½" + ⅞" = 2⅜" wide

Multiple bias strip unit = 1½" + 1⅛" = 2⅝" wide

2. Cut bias squares that are ⅞" larger than the finished size.

Example:

2" + ⅞" = 2⅞" parent bias squares

3. Cut the parent bias squares once diagonally to yield two mirror-image side-by-sides as shown above.

Susan's Southern Star

Finished Size: 34" x 34"

Finished Block Size: 8"

Color photo on page 21

This warm-up project includes cutting bias strips, bias squares, and side-by-sides. Pay careful attention to the pressing directions so that all the seams butt and the pieces fit together well. I used four gold prints in my quilt to add twinkle to the stars.

Materials: 44"-wide fabric

4 squares, each 11" x 11", of a different gold print

¼ yd. gold, large-scale floral

⅜ yd. red plaid

½ yd. green print

1⅛ yds. black print

⅜ yd. for binding

1¼ yds. for backing

Color Key

Golds

Gold floral

Red plaid

Green

Black

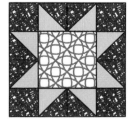

Star
Make 4.

Cutting: All measurements include ¼"-wide seam allowances.

From each of the 4 gold prints, cut:
1 square, 10" x 10", for bias squares.

From the gold, large-scale floral, cut:
1 strip, 4½" x 42"; crosscut into:
    4 squares, each 4½" x 4½", for Star centers;
    4 bars, each 2½" x 4½", for pieced border;
    4 squares, each 2½" x 2½", for pieced border corners.

From the red plaid, cut:
2 strips, each 4⅞" x 42"; crosscut into:
    10 squares, each 4⅞" x 4⅞", for sashings and border.

From the green print, cut:
1 strip, 12" x 42"; crosscut into:
    1 strip, 12" x 24", for side-by-side strip unit;
    1 square, 4½" x 4½", for sashing center;
    4 squares, each 1½" x 1½", for border corner squares;

2 strips, each 1½" x 42"; crosscut into:
    4 strips, each 1½" x 20½", for inner border.

From the black print, cut:
1 strip, 12" x 42"crosscut into:
    1 strip, 12" x 24", for side-by-side strip unit;
    28 squares, each 2½" x 2½", for blocks and
      pieced border;

4 squares, each 10" x 10", for bias squares;

1 strip 4⅞" x 42"; crosscut into:
    2 squares, each 4⅞" x 4⅞, for sashings and
      border;
    8 squares, each 1½" x 1½", for border corner
      squares;

6 strips, each 1½" x42", for middle and outer borders.

From the fabric for binding, cut:
4 strips, each 2" x 42".

Piecing the Blocks
Press seam allowances in the direction of the arrows unless otherwise instructed.

Follow the directions on pages 47–48 for cutting Method One bias strips.
1. Pair each black 10" square with a gold 10" square, right sides together. Cut the stacked squares into 2½"-wide bias strips and sew like-sized strips together along one long edge into bias-strip pairs. Sew the long black and gold bias strip pairs into Bias Strip Unit I as shown.

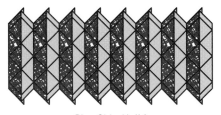

Bias Strip Unit I
Press seams to the right.
Cut 38 bias squares.

Sew the short black and gold bias strips into Bias Strip Unit II as shown.

Bias Strip Unit II
Press seams to the left.
Cut 23 bias squares.

Cut the bias squares as shown. You will cut a total 61 bias squares, each 2½" x 2½", from Bias Strip Units I and II, but you need only 56. Divide the squares so that 28 have seams pressed toward the black, and 28 have seams pressed toward the gold.

Cut 28.   Cut 28.

2. Pair 16 bias squares, all with seams pressed in the direction of the arrows as shown for Unit I, and stitch. Pair 16 bias squares, all with seams pressed in the direction of the arrows as shown for Unit II, and stitch. Set aside the remaining 24 gold/black bias squares to use in the pieced border.

Unit I
Make 8.

Unit II
Make 8.

3. Sew a black 2½" square to each side of 4 of the Unit I bias-square pairs, and 4 of the Unit II bias-square pairs.

Unit I
Make 8.

Unit II
Make 8.

4. Assemble 2 types of Star blocks, using the units made in step 3, the remaining bias-square pairs, and the 4½" gold floral squares. Use Unit I bias-square pairs to make Block A, and Unit II pairs to make Block B. Press seams joining the rows together to one side.

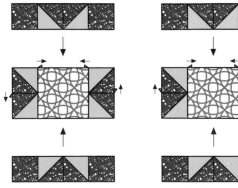

Block A
Make 2.
Use only Unit I
bias-square pairs.

Block B
Make 2.
Use only Unit II
bias-square pairs.

Piecing the Sashing

Follow the directions on pages 48–49 for cutting Method Two bias strips.

1. Stack the green and black 12" x 24" strips together, right sides up. Cut the stack completely into 4¼"-wide bias strips. Sew the strips into a bias strip unit as shown. Cut 12 bias squares, each 4⅞" x 4⅞". You need 6 with the seams pressed toward the green and 6 with the seams pressed toward the black.

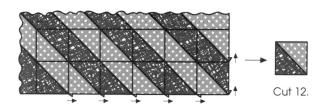

Cut 12.

Note: You will have 1 leftover corner strip each of black and green. If you need 1 or 2 more bias squares, sew the leftover black and green corner bias strips together along the long edges and press. Cut the necessary bias squares from this extra single strip unit.

2. Cut the green and black bias squares once diagonally to yield 24 side-by-sides, half with seams pressed toward the green and half with seams pressed toward the black.

3. Sort the side-by-sides into 4 groups by mirror image and pressing direction, indicated by the arrows.

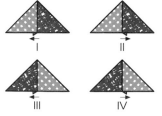

I   II
III   IV

4. Cut the 2 black and 10 red 4⅞" squares once diagonally to create 4 black half-square triangles and 20 red half-square triangles.

5. Using 4 each of the red and black half-square triangles and 2 each of the 4 different types of green and black side-by-sides, assemble the sashing patches as shown. Reserve the remaining half-square triangles and side-by-sides for the middle pieced border.

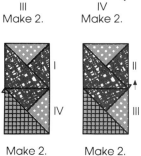

I
Make 2.

II
Make 2.

III
Make 2.

IV
Make 2.

6. Join the black and red sashing patches to make 4 pieced sashings. Sew a black patch I to a red patch IV. Sew a black patch II to a red patch III.

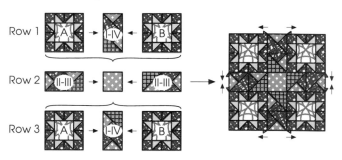

I   II
IV   III
Make 2.   Make 2.

Assembling and Finishing the Quilt Top

1. Arrange the Star blocks, 4½" green square, and 4 pieced sashings as shown. Stitch in 3 rows. Press seams in Rows 1 and 3 toward the Star blocks. Press seams in Row 2 toward the center square.

Row 1 A I-IV B
Row 2 II-III II-III
Row 3 A I-IV B

2. Join the rows to complete the quilt center and press.

3. Refer to the directions on page 94 for measuring, cutting, and attaching borders with corner squares. Sew 2 of the green 1½" x 20½" inner border strips to opposite sides of the quilt top. Press seams toward the border strips.

4. Sew a 1½" corner square to each end of the 2 remaining border strips; press seams toward the border strips. Sew the border strips to the top and bottom of the quilt top; press seams toward the border strips.

5. Measure, trim, and sew 4 of the 1½" x 42" black-print border strips to the quilt top as described for the inner border, adding a 1½" corner square to each end of the top and bottom border strips. Press seams toward the black border. Reserve 2 border strips for the outer border.

6. Sew the remaining I, II, III, and IV side-by-sides to the 16 red half-square triangles to make 4 of each patch type.

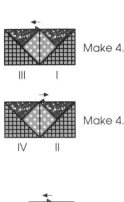

7. Join patches I and III as shown. Join patches II and IV as shown.

Make 4.

III   I

Make 4.

IV   II

8. Sew 8 gold/black bias squares into 4 pairs. Be sure to pair bias squares that are pressed in opposite directions as shown in the diagram.

Make 4.

9. Sew a 2½" black square to each side of each pair.

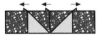

10. Sew 2 bias squares to each gold floral bar. Be careful to orient the triangle points as shown.

Make 4.

11. Sew each unit made in step 9 to a bar unit made in step 10.

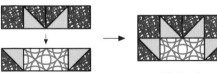

Make 4.

12. Assemble 4 pieced border units as shown. Press seams to one side.

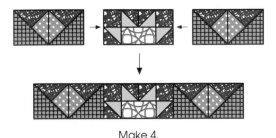

Make 4.

13. Before attaching the pieced border, measure the quilt top. It should measure 25" x 25". If it is larger or smaller, the pieced border strips will not fit. You can ease minor differences, but if they are over 1", adjust the seams in the pieced border, making a few of them slightly wider or narrower so the border strip will fit the quilt top. Sew 2 pieced borders to the sides of the quilt top and press seams toward the black middle border.

14. Using the remaining 8 gold/black bias squares, 4 gold floral 2½" squares, and 4 black 2½" squares, make four-patch corner squares as shown.

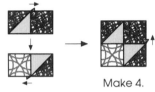

Make 4.

15. Sew a four-patch corner square to each end of the 2 remaining pieced border units, positioning them as shown. Sew the pieced border strips with corner squares to the top and bottom of the quilt top.

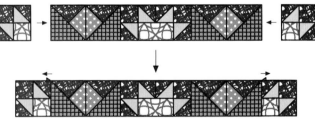

Make 2.

16. Cut the 2 remaining 1½" x 42" black border strips in half crosswise. Sew a leftover piece from step 5 to each half strip to make 4 pieced border strips. Measure, cut, and sew the pieced 1½" black outer border strips to the quilt top as described for the inner border, adding a 1½" corner square to each end of the top and bottom border strips. Press seams toward the outer border.

17. Layer the completed quilt top with batting and backing; baste.

18. Quilt as desired.

19. Bind the edges, following the directions on pages 95–96.

55

Birds in the Air

Finished Size: 51" x 59½"

Finished Block Size: 6"

Color photos on pages 21–22

This Birds in the Air quilt lends itself well to the use of scraps. The fabric requirements given here are for pieces that yield two blocks for every dark and light pair of fabrics. Make as many blocks as you wish and trade fabrics or blocks with friends to make a friendship quilt. Directions are for a diagonally set, repetitive quilt.

Materials: 44"-wide fabric

8" x 16" piece from each of 36 assorted dark fabrics

8" x 12" piece from each of 36 assorted light fabrics

10" x 10" square from each of 6 assorted light fabrics

6" x 6" square from each of 2 different light fabrics

½ yd. for binding

4 yds. for backing

Color Key

Darks

Lights

Birds in the Air
Make 72.

Cutting: All measurements include ¼"-wide seam allowances.

From each of the 36 assorted dark fabrics, cut:
2 squares, each 6⅞" x 6⅞", for bias squares and large half-square triangles.

From each of the 36 assorted light fabrics, cut:
1 square, 6⅞" x 6⅞", for bias squares;

2 squares, each 2⅞" x 2⅞", for block triangles.

From each of the 6 assorted lights, cut:
1 square, 9¾" x 9¾", for side setting triangles.

From each of the 2 different lights, cut:
1 square, 5½" x 5½", for corner triangles.

From the fabric for binding, cut:
6 strips, each 2" x 42".

Piecing the Blocks

Press seam allowances in the direction of the arrows unless otherwise instructed.

Follow the directions on pages 47–48 for cutting Method One bias strips.

1. With right sides together, pair a dark 6⅞" square with a light 6⅞" square. Make 36 pairs.

2. Cut each pair in half diagonally and then cut into 2½"-wide bias strips. Sew the strips together on the long edges and press seams toward the light. Sew corner triangles together on long edges and press seam toward the dark.

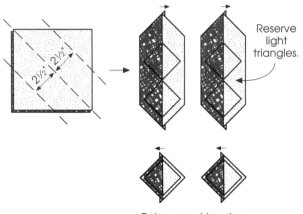

Reserve light triangles.

Pair corner triangles.

3. Cut 2 bias squares, each 2½" x 2½", from each of the long bias strip units, and 1 bias square, 2½" x 2½", from each of the triangle pairs. Set aside the 2 light triangles left over from the bias strip edges for use in step 5.

4. Cut each remaining dark 6⅞" square once diagonally to make 2 half-square triangles. Following the directions on pages 10–11, nub the triangles to measure 6½"; set aside.

5. Cut the 2 light 2⅞" squares once diagonally to make 4 half-square triangles. Nub the triangles to measure 2½". Resize and nub the 2 light leftover triangles from step 3 to measure 2½". See page 11 for resizing triangles.

2½"

Resize and nub to 2½".

6. Using 2 matching large dark half-square triangles, 6 bias squares to match the dark half-square triangles, and 6 matching small light half-square triangles, assemble 2 Birds in the Air blocks. Use bias squares pressed to the light for top row and a bias square pressed to the dark for middle row.

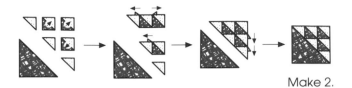

Make 2.

7. Make 2 blocks from each of the remaining 35 dark and light combinations.

Assembling and Finishing the Quilt Top

1. Cut the 6 light 9¾" squares twice diagonally to make 24 side setting triangles. You will use 22 of these slightly oversized triangles and trim them later. Cut the 2 light 5½" squares once diagonally to make 4 corner triangles.

2. Arrange the blocks as shown below, adding the side setting triangles. Join the blocks and triangles in diagonal rows, alternating the pressing direction from row to row.

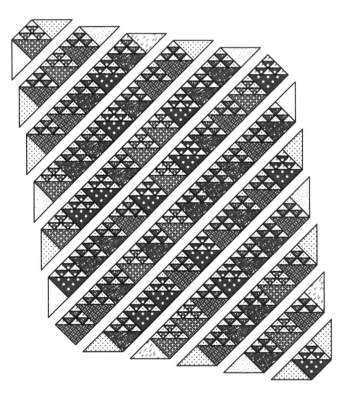

3. Join the rows to complete the quilt top and add the corner triangles last. Trim the quilt edges to ¼" from the block points (page 94).

4. Layer the completed quilt top with batting and backing; baste.

5. Quilt as desired.

6. Bind the edges, following the directions on pages 95–96.

Turkey Tracks

Finished Size: 58" x 58"

Finished Block Size: 11½"

Color photo on page 23

This quilt is easy to make in short spurts over a long period of time. Collect fat quarters* of darks and lights to combine. Each combination yields two completed blocks that are the color reverse of each other. It is so easy!

*A fat quarter of fabric measures 18" x 22" and is sold precut in fabric stores. Of course, you can cut one from fabric you already have.

Materials: 44"-wide fabric

8 dark fat quarters

8 light fat quarters

⅜ yd. light print for inner border

1 yd. medium print for outer border

½ yd. for binding

3¾ yds. for backing

Color Key

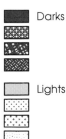

Darks

Lights

Medium

Block A
Make 8.

Block B
Make 8.

Cutting: All measurements include ¼"-wide seam allowances.

From each dark and each light fat quarter, cut:
1 square, 10" x 10", for bias squares;

4 strips, each 1½" x 10", for block sashing;

4 squares, each 1½" x 1½", for block sashing corners;

4 bars, each 2" x 4½", for block piecing;

1 square, 2" x 2", for block center;

4 squares, each 2½" x 2½", for block corners;

2 squares, each 4⅞" x 4⅞"; cut once diagonally to yield 4 half-square triangles for block piecing.

From the light print for the inner border, cut:
5 strips, each 2" x 42".

From the medium print for the outer border, cut:
6 strips, each 5" x 42".

From the fabric for binding, cut:
6 strips, each 2" x 42".

Piecing the Blocks
Press seam allowances in the direction of the arrows unless otherwise instructed.

Follow the directions on pages 47–48 for cutting Method One bias strips. Decide which dark print will go with which light print and then keep all the pieces cut from those 2 prints together. Each dark/light combination yields 1 Block A and 1 Block B.

1. With right sides together, pair a 10" dark square with a 10" light square.

2. Cut the pair of squares in half diagonally and then cut into 2½"-wide bias strips. Sew the resulting bias strips together in light/dark pairs along the long edge. Cut a total of 8 bias squares, each 2⅞" x 2⅞", from the bias strip units. You will have 4 pressed toward the dark and 4 pressed toward the light.

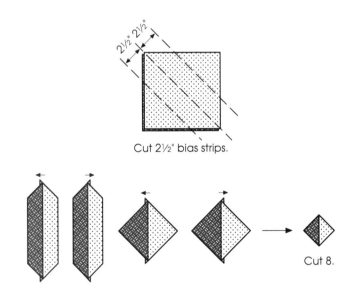

Cut 2½" bias strips.

Cut 8.

3. Cut the bias squares once diagonally to yield 16 side-by-side triangles.

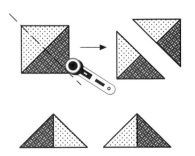

4. Sew 2 side-by-side triangles to each of the 4 light and 4 dark 2½" squares. Carefully position the dark and light triangles of the side-by-sides with the dark and light squares as shown. Block A has side-by-sides with its seams pressed toward the light and Block B has side-by-sides with its seams pressed toward the dark.

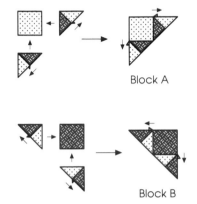

Block A

Block B

5. Sew Block A side-by-side units from step 4 to the dark half-square triangles, and the Block B side-by-side units to the light half-square triangles. Press seams toward the large half-square triangles.

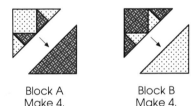

Block A
Make 4.

Block B
Make 4.

6. Sew a Block A unit to opposite sides of a light 2" x 4½" bar. Sew a Block B unit to opposite sides of a dark 2" x 4½" bar. Press seams toward the bars.

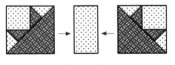

Block A
Make 2 for each block.

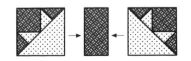

Block B
Make 2 for each block.

7. Sew a light 2" x 4½" bar to opposite sides of a dark 2" square. Sew a dark 2" x 4½" bar to opposite sides of a light 2" square. Press the seams toward the bars.

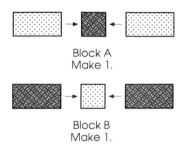

Block A
Make 1.

Block B
Make 1.

8. Sew the Block A units to the light center bar unit, and the Block B units to the dark center bar unit. Press seams toward the center bar units.

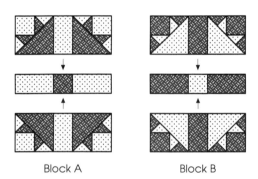

Block A   Block B

9. Sew a dark 1½" x 10" sashing strip to each side of each Block A. Sew a light sashing strip to each side of each Block B.
10. Sew a 1½" light square to each end of a dark sashing strip. You will need 2 for Block A. Sew to the top and bottom of Block A. Sew a 1½" dark square to each end of a light sashing strip. You will need 2 for Block B. Sew to the top and bottom of Block B.

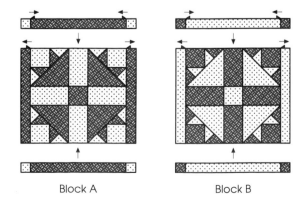

Block A   Block B

11. Make 2 blocks from each of the remaining 7 dark/light combinations.

Assembling and Finishing the Quilt Top

1. Arrange the blocks in 4 rows of 4 blocks each as shown in the quilt plan on page 57 and stitch. If the seams at the sashing corners do not match, rotate 1 block once to the right or to the left until the seams butt against each other.
2. Cut 1 of the light print 2" x 42" inner border strips into 4 equal strips. Sew a quarter strip to one end of each remaining 42"-long strip; press seams in either direction.
3. Refer to the directions on page 94 for measuring, cutting, and attaching borders with straight-cut corners. Trim 2 inner border strips to match the center length measurement of the quilt top and sew to opposite sides; press seams toward the border.
4. Trim the other 2 inner border strips to match the center width measurement of the quilt top and sew to the top and bottom. Press seams toward the border strips.
5. Cut 2 of the medium print 5" x 42" outer border strips in half crosswise and sew a half strip to one end of each of the remaining 42"-long strips. Press seams in either direction. Measure, cut, and sew the outer border strips to the quilt top as described for the inner border. Press seams toward the outer border.
6. Layer the completed quilt top with batting and backing; baste.
7. Quilt as desired.
8. Bind the edges, following the directions on pages 95–96.

Mosaic Sparkler

Finished Size: 48" x 64"

Finished Block Size: 8"

Color photo on page 24

The Mosaic Sparkler quilt uses a color-family recipe. I used many prints from only two color families: violet and teal. Choose two colors and then select fabrics from each. Choose big prints, plaids, small prints, and different shades and values within each color family. Don't try to match too closely.

I made a pieced binding of leftover teal prints. A 2" x 20" strip from each of the 12 prints will yield more than enough binding for the quilt.

Materials: 44"-wide fabric

⅜ yd. each of 12 assorted teal prints

8 fat quarters (18" x 22") of assorted violet prints

12 fat quarters (18" x 22") of assorted light prints that coordinate with the violet and teal

½ yd. for binding (if not making pieced binding from leftovers)

4⅛ yds. for backing*

*Or make a pieced backing from the leftover 10" triangles. (See "Tip" on page 61.)

Color Key

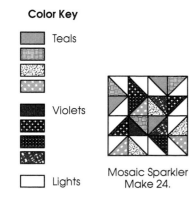

Teals

Violets

Lights

Mosaic Sparkler
Make 24.

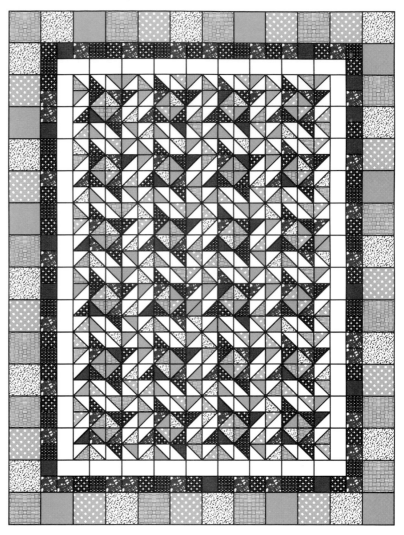

Cutting: All measurements include ¼"-wide seam allowances.

From each of the 12 assorted teal prints, cut:
1 piece, 10" x 21", for bias strip units;

5 squares, each 4½" x 4½", for outer pieced border.

From each of the 8 assorted violet prints, cut:
1 piece, 10" x 21", for bias strip units;

12 squares, each 2½" x 2½", for middle pieced border.

From each of the 12 assorted light prints, cut:
1 piece, 10" x 21", for bias strip units;

4 rectangles, each 2½" x 4½", for inner pieced border.

From the fabric for binding, cut:
6 strips, each 2" x 42".

Piecing the Blocks
Press seam allowances in the direction of the arrows unless otherwise instructed.

Follow the directions on pages 48–49 for cutting Method Two bias strips.
1. Stack 4 of the 10" x 21" pieces, right sides up. (Colors can be mixed.) Cut all 4 layers of fabric at once into 2½"-wide bias strips. Cut only 1 corner piece into bias strips and save the other for another project or the quilt back. Each piece yields the following: 3 full strips, 1 corner strip, and 1 corner triangle. Repeat for all of the remaining 10" x 21" pieces.

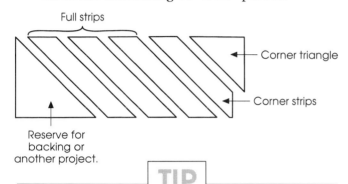

Full strips

Corner triangle

Corner strips

Reserve for backing or another project.

TIP

Use the 32 assorted 10" triangles left over from step 1 to create a pieced backing. Nub and resize the 10" triangles to 9½" (See "Resizing Half-Square Triangles" on page 11.) These 9½" nubbed triangles can now be sewn to each other or other 9½" resized triangles from your fabric collection to form pieced squares that will finish to 9". Use these and other squares and rectangles to make a free-form pieced backing. See sample pieced backings in the Gallery on pages 19, 29, and 32 for ideas.

---

2. Sort the cut strips by strip type and by color family. Stack all the violets into 3 piles: 1 stack of full strips, 1 stack of corner strips, and 1 stack of corner triangles. Repeat with the teal and light prints.
3. Assemble the following number of strip units, using 3 full strips, 1 corner strip, and 1 corner triangle *from each of the two color families.*

   8 teal/light-print strip units
   4 violet/light-print strip units
   4 violet/teal strip units

Press half of the strip units from each color combination toward one color and the other half toward the other color.

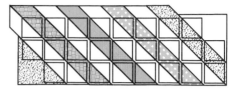

4. Cut 24 bias squares, each 2½" x 2½", from each strip unit. Group these bias squares by color and pressed-seam direction. You need the following number of bias squares:

   From the teal/light, 192 total,
   96 pressed each way;

   From the violet/light, 96 total,
   48 pressed each way;

   From the violet/teal, 96 total,
   48 pressed each way.

5. Assemble the bias squares into the 4 types of pairs as shown.

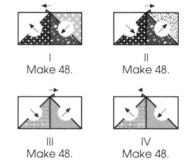

I
Make 48.

II
Make 48.

III
Make 48.

IV
Make 48.

6. Join the pairs into groups of 4. Pay attention to pressed seam direction when joining the pairs.

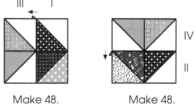

III   I

IV

II

Make 48.   Make 48.

7. Join the groups of 4 to make half blocks.

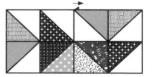

Make 48.

8. Join the half blocks to complete the Mosaic blocks. Press the final seam to one side.

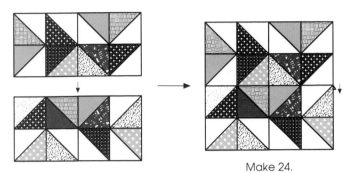

Make 24.

Assembling and Finishing the Quilt Top

1. Arrange the blocks into 6 rows of 4 blocks each. Alternate the direction of the center seam from block to block as shown in the diagram. Sew the blocks in horizontal rows. Press seams in opposite directions from row to row. Join the rows together and press.

Note: Flip seams that do not butt in the proper direction. (See "Pressing," option 1, page 12.)

Center seam of block

TIP

Do not press seams in the pieced border until you sew it to the quilt top. Then flip seams so they butt with matching quilt seams.

2. You need 42 of the 48 light 2½" x 4½" rectangles you cut for the inner pieced border. Make 2 pieced borders of 12 light 2½" x 4½" rectangles each for the sides. Placing light prints randomly, sew the rectangles along the short ends. Sew border strips to the sides, flipping seams as you go. Press seam toward the border strips.

Side Borders
Make 2.

Make 2 pieced borders of 9 light rectangles each for the top and bottom. Sew to the top and bottom of the quilt top, flipping seams to match as you go; press seams toward the border strips.

Top and Bottom Borders
Make 2.

3. Make 2 pieced borders of 26 violet 2½" squares each for the sides and 2 pieced borders of 20 violet squares each for the top and bottom. Arrange the squares randomly. You will have 4 left over from the 96 you cut. Attach the sides first and then the top and bottom border strips as in step 2; press seams toward the middle border.

4. Make 2 pieced border strips of 14 teal 4½" squares each for the sides and 2 pieced borders of 12 teal squares each for the top and bottom. There will be 8 left over. Attach border strips to the sides first and then to the top and bottom; press seams toward the outer border.

5. Layer the completed quilt top with batting and backing; baste.

6. Quilt as desired.

7. Bind the edges, following the directions on pages 95–96.

Striped Squares and Triangles

CUTTING AND ASSEMBLING STRIPED SQUARES

Often, pieced squares have stripes across the diagonal of the square. Cut striped squares, following the same Method Two bias strip-piecing directions in Section Two. Like bias squares, striped squares are cut ½" larger than the desired finished size. Learn how to quick-piece and cut different types of striped squares in this section.

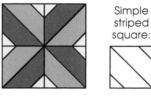

Simple striped square:

King's Cross

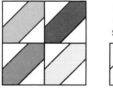

Center striped square:

Indian Hatchet

Offset striped square:

Land of the Midnight Sun

There are two types of strips in striped squares: center strips and outer strips. There can be only two outer strips, which form the corners of the square. There can be any number of center strips.

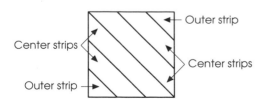

Center strips —
Outer strip →
← Outer strip
← Center strips

Cut the center strips to the finished size plus ½" for seam allowances. When planning a striped square, make the center strip units in easily measured ⅛" increments. Round up any odd measurements of the outer strips to the nearest ⅛" increment before adding seam allowances.

Assembling a Bias Strip Unit for a Striped Square

Striped squares are usually cut from Method Two multiple bias strip units.

1. Cut center strips the desired finished width plus ½" for seam allowances.
2. Cut outer strips the finished width plus ⅞". Round up the finished width to the nearest ⅛".

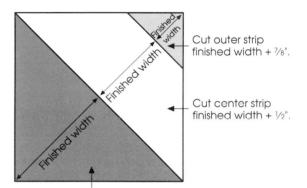

Cut outer strip finished width + ⅞".

Cut center strip finished width + ½".

Cut outer strip finished width + ⅞".

3. Cut bias strips for striped squares from yardage, not squares, in the same fashion as shown for Method Two bias strip units on pages 48–49. Do not layer the strip fabrics unless cutting all the strips the same width.
4. When sewing the strips together, offset the strips and sew from top to bottom as for regular bias strip units. Only full bias strips are used in bias strip units for striped squares.

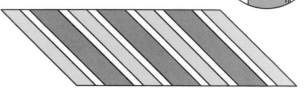

Note: After cutting the bias strips, you will have two large corner pieces left over. If bias squares are used in the quilt, these leftover triangles can be paired with other large triangles and cut into bias strips for Method One bias strip units as shown on pages 47–48. These two large triangles are the equivalent of one large square cut in half diagonally.

Cutting Striped Squares

1. Cut striped squares from the bias strip unit, centering the diagonal line of the Bias Square ruler over the center seam line of the striped square. If there is no center seam line, as in the center striped square, center the diagonal line over the middle of the strip, marking a center line on the fabric strip if necessary.

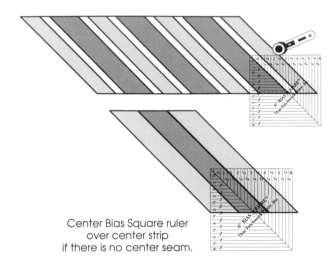

Center Bias Square ruler
over center strip
if there is no center seam.

2. When striped squares are cut from the strip unit, small waste rectangles are left over between the pairs, and tiny fabric slivers are left over between each striped square. These slivers are not shown in the strip-unit diagrams. The leftover triangles on the strip-unit edges can be used for Method One bias strip piecing, or resized and used as striped triangles in another quilt pattern.

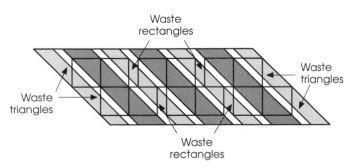

Waste
rectangles

Waste
triangles

Waste
triangles

Waste
rectangles

CUTTING AND ASSEMBLING
STRIPED TRIANGLES

Just as bias squares may be cut into side-by-side triangles, striped squares can be cut into striped triangles. Cut the striped square in half diagonally, perpendicular to the strip seams. To make striped half-square triangles, add ⅞" to the short edge of the finished triangle size to determine the parent striped-square size. To make striped quarter-square triangles, add 1¼" to the long edge of the finished triangle size to determine the parent striped-square size.

Parent striped squares may be cut from either bias or straight-grain strip units, depending on where you want the straight of grain.

Note that striped triangles cut from some striped squares are mirror-image units and are not interchangeable.

Below are some examples of striped triangles and the parent striped squares from which they are cut.

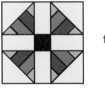

Simple
striped
triangle:

All Dressed Up

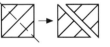

Offset-
striped
triangle:

Dutch Windmill

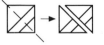

Center-
striped
triangle:

Sparkler

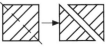

Cutting Strips for Striped Triangles

1. Cut all interior strips to the desired finished width plus ½".
2. To account for the extra seam, cut the outer strips the finished width (rounded up) plus 1⅛". If you'd like a little more "elbow room" with your outer strip widths, you may add 1¼" to the finished width.

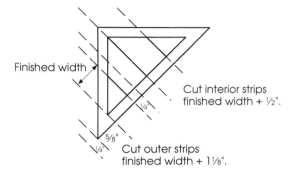

Finished width

Cut interior strips
finished width + ½".

Cut outer strips
finished width + 1⅛".

Striped Triangle Variations

Striped triangles are usually cut perpendicular to the stripes, while the triangle variations shown below are cut from the striped square directly through and parallel to the center stripe. For center-striped, quarter-square triangles, the striped square is cut twice diagonally to yield four striped triangles.

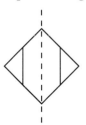
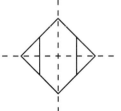
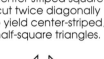

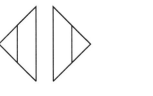

Center-striped square cut in half through center stripe to yield center-striped, half-square triangles.

Center-striped square cut twice diagonally to yield center-striped, half-square triangles.

As a result, there are a few differences in figuring strip width and striped-square size.

To cut strips for center-striped, half-square triangles:

1. Cut the center strip 1" wider than twice the desired finished width for one triangle, allowing for ¼"-wide seams on either side of

the strip and ¼" on either side of the center cut. Refer to the striped triangle below. The finished width of the center strip is 1". This measurement is doubled, and 1" is added for the four seams, to equal a 3"-wide strip.

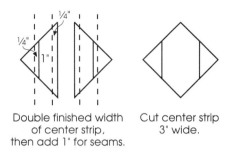

Double finished width of center strip, then add 1" for seams.

Cut center strip 3" wide.

2. Cut outer strips the finished width plus 1". Since you do not cut across the outer strips, they are calculated the same as for striped squares.
3. For seam allowances, add ⅞" to the desired finished size when cutting the parent striped square for center-striped, half-square triangles.

To cut strips for center-striped, quarter-square triangles:

1. Cut the center strip as for the center-striped, half-square triangle (twice the desired finished width plus 1" for seams).
2. Cut outer strips the finished width plus 1⅛". (Add 1¼" if you'd like more elbow room.)

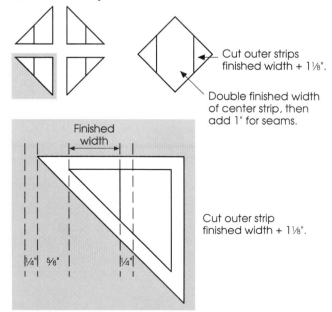

Cut outer strips finished width + 1⅛".

Double finished width of center strip, then add 1" for seams.

Finished width

Cut outer strip finished width + 1⅛".

3. Cut the parent striped square for center-striped, quarter-square triangles 1¼" larger than the desired finished size of the long edge of the striped triangle, since it is cut twice diagonally.

Warm-up
PROJECT

Double Star

Finished Size: 45 ½" x 55 ½"

Finished Block Size: 10"

Color photo on page 25

I've taught this quilt in many workshops. It goes together quickly and easily, and the different color placements that result are intriguing. It is 45½" wide, making it a good candidate for a pieced backing. One quilter's backing solution was to add 3"-wide border strips to a 39½" x 49½" piece of backing fabric.

Materials: 44"-wide fabric

1¾ yds. black print

¾ yd. pink print

1 yd. rose print

1 yd. gray print

½ yd. for binding

3½ yds. for backing

Color Key

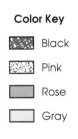

Black

Pink

Rose

Gray

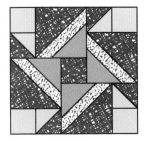

Double Star
Make 12.

Cutting: All measurements include ¼"-wide seam allowances.

From the black print, cut:
2 pieces, each 11" x 42", for striped-square, bias strip units;

1 piece, 11" x 42"; crosscut into:
    1 piece, 11" x 23", for striped-square, bias strip units;
    12 squares, each 2½" x 2½", for block centers;

5 strips, each 5" x 42", for outer border.

From the pink print, cut:
2 pieces, each 11" x 42", for striped-square, bias strip units.

From the rose print, cut:
2 pieces, each 11" x 42", for striped-square, bias strip units;

5 strips, each 1¾" x 42", for middle border.

From the gray print, cut:
1 piece, 11" x 42"; crosscut into:
    3 squares, each 11" x 11", for bias strip units;

3 strips, each 2½" x 42"; crosscut into:
    48 squares, each 2½" x 2½", for blocks;

4 strips, each 2½" x 42", for inner border.

From the fabric for binding, cut:
6 strips, each 2" x 42".

Piecing the Blocks
Press seam allowances in the direction of the arrows unless otherwise instructed.

1. Cut the following full bias strips from the indicated pieces, following directions on page 48:

Fabric	No. of Pieces	Dimensions	Full Bias Strips from Each Piece	Strip Width
Black	2	11" x 42"	10	4"
	1	11" x 23"	2	4"
Rose	2	11" x 42"	16	2¾"
Pink	2	11" x 42"	24	1⅝"

Set aside the leftover black corner pieces to pair with the gray 11" squares in step 4. Save the pink and rose corner pieces for another project.

2. Using the black, rose, and pink bias strips, assemble 4 striped-square strip units as shown. Be sure to keep the strips in order.

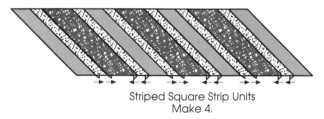

Striped Square Strip Units
Make 4.

3. Using a Bias Square ruler, cut a total of 48 striped squares, each 4½" x 4½", from the bias strip units. Place the diagonal line of the ruler on the seam between the black and pink strips.

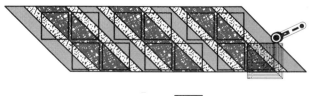

Cut a total of
48 striped squares.

4. Cut the gray 11" squares in half diagonally to yield 6 large triangles. Pair the gray triangles with the 6 leftover black corner pieces from step 1. These may not fit exactly, so pair them, right sides together, with the bias edges aligned. Cut 2½"-wide bias strips from these pairs.

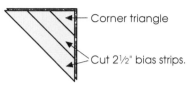

— Corner triangle

Cut 2½" bias strips.

5. Sew the bias-strip pairs together on their long edges. Also, sew together 3 pairs of the small corner triangles, left over after cutting the bias strips. Join like-size bias strip units into multiple bias strip units.

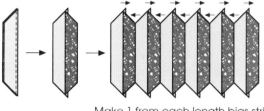

Make 1 from each length bias strip.

Sew 3 pairs of
corner triangles together.

6. Cut a total of 48 bias squares, each 2½" x 2½", from the multiple bias strip units and corner triangle pairs.

7. Sew a 2½" gray square to each of the 48 bias squares as shown.

8. Sew a 4½" striped square from step 3 to each bias-square unit made in step 7.

9. Sew a striped-square/bias-square unit to a 2½" black square as shown, using a partial seam. Refer to the directions for partial seams on page 15.

10. Join a second striped-square unit to the center unit.

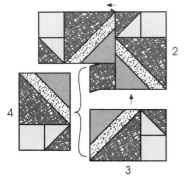

11. Add 2 more striped-square units to the center in numerical order, pressing seams toward the previously added unit. Complete the block by finishing the half seam.

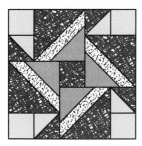

Double Star
Make 12.

Assembling and Finishing the Quilt Top

1. Arrange the blocks into 4 horizontal rows of 3 blocks each, as shown in the quilt plan on page 66. Stitch; press seams in opposite directions from row to row.
2. Join the rows to complete the quilt center. Press seams to one side.
3. Refer to the directions on page 94 for measuring, cutting, and attaching borders with corner squares. Trim 2 gray 2½" x 42" inner border strips to match the center length measurement of the quilt top for the side borders. Trim the other 2 gray inner border strips to match the center width measurement for the top and bottom borders. Sew the side borders to opposite sides of the quilt top; press seams toward the border.
4. Cut 4 corner squares, each 2½" x 2½", from leftover gray strips, and sew a square to each end of the top and bottom border strips. Press seams toward the border strips. Sew the border strips to the top and bottom of the quilt top; press seams toward the border.
5. Cut 1 rose 1¾" x 42" middle border strip in half crosswise and sew a half strip to one end of 2 of the 42"-long strips for the side borders. Measure, cut, and sew the middle border as described for the inner border. Cut 4 corner squares, each 1¾" x 1¾", from leftover rose strips.
6. Cut 1 black 5" x 42" outer border strip in half crosswise and sew a half strip to one end of 2 of the 42"-long strips for the side borders. Measure, cut, and sew the 5" black border strips as described for the inner border. Cut 4 corner squares, each 5" x 5", from leftover black strips.
7. Layer the completed quilt top with batting and backing; baste.
8. Quilt as desired.
9. Bind the edges, following the directions on pages 95–96.

Spools

Finished Size: 56" x 64"

Finished Block Size: 4"

Color photos on pages 28–29

One of my pattern testers commented that a beginner would be thrilled with the construction ease of this quilt, while a more experienced quilter would have a great time playing with the color options. This quilt pattern is a breeze to assemble, and the border is constructed at the same time as the rest of the quilt. Use leftover fabric to make a pieced backing.

Materials: 44"-wide fabric

⅜ yd. each of 5 blue prints

⅜ yd. each of 5 red prints

⅝ yd. each of 6 light prints

½ yd. for binding

4 yds. for backing

Color Key

Blues

Reds

Lights

Block A
Make 60.

Block B
Make 60.

Cutting: All measurements include ¼"-wide seam allowances.

From each of the 5 blues and 5 reds, cut:
1 piece, 11" x 42", for striped-square, bias strip units.

From each of 5 light prints, cut:
1 piece, 11" x 42", for striped-square, bias strip units;

1 strip, 4½" x 42"; crosscut into:
    8 squares, each 4½" x 4½", for the inner border.

From the sixth light print, cut:
3 squares, each 11" x 11", for side-by-side, bias strip units;

1 strip, 4½" x 42"; crosscut into:
    8 squares, each 4½" x 4½", for the inner border.

From the fabric for binding, cut:
7 strips, each 2" x 42".

Piecing the Blocks

Press seam allowances in the direction of the arrows unless otherwise instructed.

Assembling Striped Squares

Refer to the directions for making striped squares on pages 63–64.

1. Sort all red and blue 11" x 42" pieces into stacks of 3 or 4, right sides facing up.
2. From each stack of fabric, cut 3 sets of bias strips, each 4" wide. Cut 4 sets of bias strips, each 2⅝" wide. Set aside the 11" corners from each 11" x 42" piece for use later.

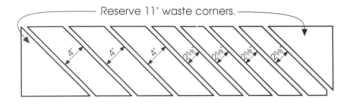

3. Stack the light-print pieces in the same fashion and cut 12 sets of 1⅞"-wide bias strips from each stack. Set aside the 11" corners for use later.
4. Sort all bias strips by width and color family.
5. Assemble 5 striped-square strip units each of Versions A and B, using the various widths of bias strips. Use 4"-wide blue strips and 2⅝"-wide red strips for Unit A; use 4"-wide red strips and 2⅝"-wide blue strips for Unit B. Cut 12 striped squares, each 4½" x 4½", from each of the 10 strip units as shown.

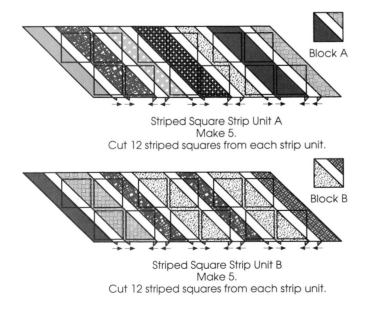

Block A

Striped Square Strip Unit A
Make 5.
Cut 12 striped squares from each strip unit.

Block B

Striped Square Strip Unit B
Make 5.
Cut 12 striped squares from each strip unit.

Assembling Side-by-Sides for the Border

1. Pair each of the 8 red and 8 blue 11" corner pieces right sides together with a light 11" corner piece and cut 4"-wide bias strips from each triangle pair. Set aside the small corner triangles left over after cutting the bias strips, to use later.

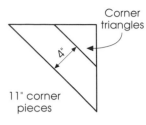

Corner triangles

11" corner pieces

2. Sew all strips along the long edges. Press all seams away from the light prints.
3. Join the red-and-light print pairs and the blue-and-light print pairs into 2 separate multiple bias strip units as shown. Cut 23 bias squares, each 4⅞" x 4⅞", from each bias strip unit. Cut the bias squares once diagonally to yield a total of 92 side-by-side triangles.

Multiple Bias Strip Units.
Make 1 blue and light.
Make 1 red and light.
Cut 23 bias squares from each bias strip unit.

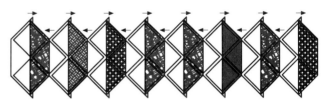

Note: You still need 5 red/light print and 5 blue/light print 4⅞" bias squares to cut into side-by-sides. Sort through the reserved small corner pieces from step 1 for 5 red, 5 blue, and 10 light triangles that measure no less than 5⅜" on the short sides. If you cannot find enough triangles of minimum size, cut some from the leftover red and blue 11" corner pieces as shown. There are enough assorted light-print scraps to cut a few 5½" squares, which can then be cut in half diagonally.

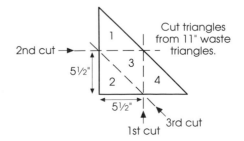

4. Pair each red and blue triangle with a light triangle and sew on the diagonal. Cut a 4⅞" bias square from each pair. Cut the 10 bias squares once diagonally to yield 20 side-by-sides.

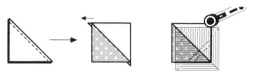

Sew 5⅜" waste triangles together; cut them into 4⅞" bias squares.

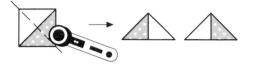

5. Sew the red/light print side-by-sides into squares as shown and press. Repeat with the blue/light print side-by-sides.

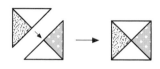

Make 28 of each color combination.

Assembling and Finishing the Quilt Top

1. Arrange the striped squares into 2 rows of 10 striped squares each, alternating Blocks A and B as shown below. Sew the units together, butting diagonal seam intersections.
2. Add a 4½" light print square and a side-by-side unit to each end of each row. Carefully position each side-by-side unit according to color and row.

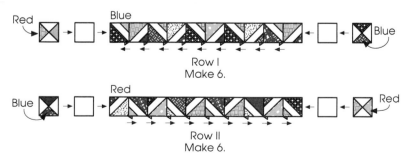

Row I
Make 6.

Row II
Make 6.

3. Sew a Row I to the top of each Row II. Make 6 pairs. Join the pairs to make the quilt top. Press seams to one side.

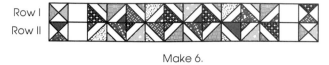

Row I
Row II

Make 6.

4. Beginning with a red/light print unit on the left, sew 14 side-by-side units together as shown.

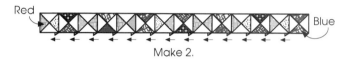

Make 2.

Sew 12 light-print squares together, adding a blue side-by-side unit to the left end, and a red side-by-side to the right end.

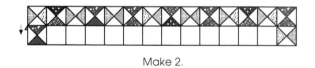

Make 2.

5. Sew each strip of squares to the bottom of a side-by-side strip and press seams to one side.

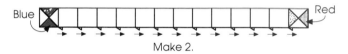

Make 2.

6. Sew a double strip made in step 5 to the top and bottom of the quilt. Refer to quilt plan on page 69 for placement.
7. Layer the completed quilt top with batting and backing; baste.
8. Quilt as desired.
9. Bind the edges, following the directions on pages 95–96.

Four Patch Ripple

Finished Size: 56" x 64"

Finished Block Size: 8"

Color photo on page 27

The block in this quilt pattern combines two smaller traditional units: a four-patch unit and a triangle unit. To add extra interest, I made the large triangles from striped triangles. The result is a diagonal wavelike feeling. Some people see the striped triangles as fish. Use exotic marine-life colors and prints to accentuate this theme if you wish.

Materials: 44"-wide fabric

¾ yd. dark red

2⅝ yds. light red print

1¾ yds. dark green

1⅛ yds. medium green

1 yd. print for outer border

½ yd. for binding

4 yds. for backing

Color Key

- Dark red
- Light red
- Dark green
- Medium green
- Print

Four Patch
Make 30.

Cutting: All measurements include ¼"-wide seam allowances.

From the dark red, cut:
9 strips, each 2½" x 42"; crosscut into:
    18 strips, each 2½" x 21", for Strip Unit I.

From the light red print, cut:
2 pieces, each 10" x 39", for bias strip units;

1 piece, 17" x 42"; crosscut into:
    2 squares, each 17" x 17", for bias strip units;

9 strips, each 2½" x 42"; crosscut into:
    18 strips, each 2½" x 21", for Strip Unit I;

5 strips, each 2⅞" x 42"; crosscut into:
    60 squares, each 2⅞" x 2⅞", for blocks;

5 strips, each 2½" x 42", for inner border.

From the dark green, cut:
2 pieces, each 17" x 42", for striped-triangle, bias strip units;

2 pieces, each 10" x 39", for bias strip units;

4 squares, each 2½" x 2½", for pieced-border corners.

From the medium green, cut:
2 pieces, each 17" x 42", for striped-triangle, bias
    strip units.

From the print for outer border, cut:
6 strips, each 4½" x 42".

From the fabric for binding, cut:
6 strips, each 2" x 42".

Piecing the Blocks
**Press seam allowances in the direction of
the arrows unless otherwise instructed.**

Four-Patch Units
1. Using the dark red and light red 2½" x 21"
   strips, assemble 18 Strip Unit I as shown. Cut
   a total of 120 segments, each 2½" wide, from
   Strip Unit I.

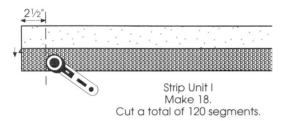

Strip Unit I
Make 18.
Cut a total of 120 segments.

2. Sew the segments into pairs to make 60 square
   four-patch units.

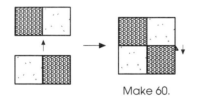

Make 60.

Triangle Units
1. Following the directions on pages 48–49 for
   cutting Method Two bias strips, cut the dark
   green and light red 10" x 39" fabric pieces into
   2½"-wide bias strips, including the corner
   pieces. Assemble 4 bias strip units as shown.
   Cut a total of 112 bias squares, each 2½" x
   2½", from the strip units. Set aside 52 bias
   squares to use for the pieced middle border.

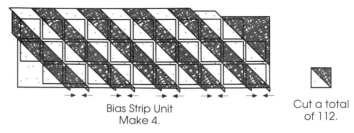

Bias Strip Unit
Make 4.

Cut a total
of 112.

2. Cut 60 light red 2⅞" squares once diagonally
   to yield 120 half-square triangles.
3. From the dark green 17" x 42" fabric pieces,
   cut a total of 10 full bias strips, each 3½" wide.
   From the medium green 17" x 42" pieces, cut
   a total of 12 full bias strips, each 2⅝" wide. Set
   aside the medium green corner pieces to use
   later. Assemble 2 striped-triangle strip units
   as shown. Cut a total of 30 striped squares,
   each 4⅞" x 4⅞", from the strip units. Center
   the diagonal line on a Bias Square ruler over
   the dark green bias strips while cutting.

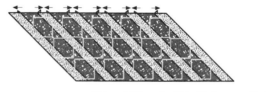

Striped-Triangle Strip Unit
Make 2.

Cut a total of
30 striped
squares.

4. Cut each striped square once diagonally,
   through the center stripe, to yield 60 striped
   half-square triangles.

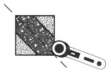

5. Sew a light red half-square triangle from step
   2 to each side of the 60 dark green/light red
   bias squares from step 1 to make 60 half units.

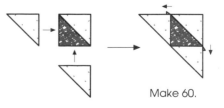

Make 60.

6. Sew a striped half-square triangle to each of the half units.

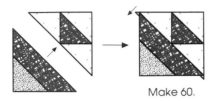

Make 60.

7. Join a square four-patch unit to a triangle unit. Orient four-patch unit so long center seam runs horizontally, with the side pressed to the light red square next to the triangle unit as shown.

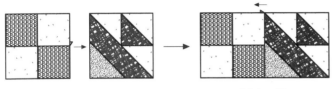

Make 60.

8. Join the half blocks to make 30 Four Patch Ripple blocks.

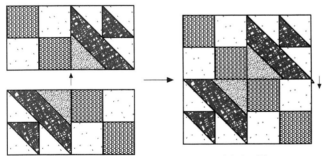

Make 30.

Assembling and Finishing the Quilt Top

1. Arrange the completed blocks into 6 horizontal rows of 5 blocks each, as shown in the quilt plan on page 72, and stitch. Press seams in opposite directions from row to row.
2. Join the rows to complete the quilt top.
3. Cut a light red 2½" x 42" inner border strip in half crosswise and sew a half strip to one end of 2 of the 42"-long strips.
4. Refer to the directions on page 94 for measuring, cutting, and attaching borders with corner squares. Trim the border strips from step 3 to match the center length measurement of the quilt top for the side borders. Trim the

remaining 2 inner border strips to match the center width measurement of the quilt top for the top and bottom borders. Sew the side borders to the sides of the quilt top; press seams toward the border.
5. Cut 4 corner squares, each 2½" x 2½", from leftover light red strips, and sew a square to each end of the top and bottom border strips. Press seams toward the border strips. Sew the strips to the top and bottom of the quilt top; press seams toward the border.
6. Cut the light red 17" squares once diagonally to yield 4 half-square triangles. With right sides together, pair the light red half-square triangles with the 4 leftover medium green 17" corner pieces set aside earlier. Cut 2½"-wide bias strips from the pairs, following the directions for Method One bias strips. (See pages 47–48.)

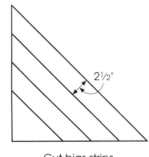

Cut bias strips.

7. Sew the bias strips together in pairs along the long edges. Make 2 multiple bias strip units of each strip size. Cut a total of 44 bias squares, each 2½" x 2½", from the bias strip units.

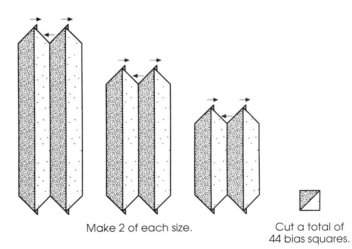

Make 2 of each size. Cut a total of 44 bias squares.

8. Using 44 of the bias squares set aside from the triangle four-patch units, sew a dark green/light red bias square to each of the 44 medium green/light red bias squares, butting the diagonal seam intersections for a sharp point.

Make 44.

9. Sew 12 of the bias-square pairs together to make the pieced middle side border. Press seams toward the dark green bias squares.

   Add a dark green/light red bias square to each end as shown for side borders below; press seams toward the end bias squares.

Note: Before attaching the pieced borders, measure the quilt top. It should measure 44½" x 52½". If it is larger or smaller, the pieced border will not fit. You can ease minor differences by adjusting the seams in the pieced border, making a few of them slightly wider or narrower so the border strips will fit the quilt top.

Sew the pieced middle border strips to opposite sides of the quilt top. Press seams toward the inner border.

10. Sew 10 bias-square pairs together to make the pieced top and bottom borders.

    Add a dark green/light red bias square and a 2½" dark green square to each end of the top and bottom border strips.

11. Sew middle pieced border strips to the top and bottom of the quilt top and press seams toward the inner border.

12. Cut 2 outer border strips in half crosswise and sew a half strip to one end of each of the remaining 42"-long strips. Measure, cut, and sew the 4" outer border strips as described for the inner border. Cut 4 corner squares, each 4½" x 4½", from leftover outer border strips.

13. Layer the completed quilt top with batting and backing; baste.

14. Quilt as desired.

15. Bind the edges, following the directions on pages 95–96.

Side Borders
Make 2.

Top and Bottom Borders
Make 2.

Shifting Winds

Finished Size: 56" x 56"

Finished Block Size: 8"

Color photo on page 26

This quilt pattern is one of my favorites. Spin the blocks in opposite directions to use both striped-triangle images.

Materials: 44"-wide fabric

2⅛ yds. black floral

1⅛ yds. brick red print

1⅜ yds. green print

1¼ yds. print for background

¾ yd. light floral print for sashing

½ yd. for binding

3½ yds. for backing

Color Key

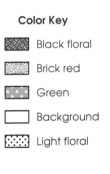

Black floral

Brick red

Green

Background

Light floral

Block A
Make 8.

Block B
Make 8.

Cutting: All measurements include ¼"-wide seam allowances.

From the black print, cut:
6 strips, each 4¼" x 42", for striped-square strip units;

4 squares, each 10" x 10", for bias strip units;

2 squares, each 12" x 12", for bias strip units;

5 strips, each 4½" x 42", for outer border.

From the brick red print, cut:
2 pieces, each 12" x 42", for striped-triangle strip units;

1 strip, 1½" x 42"; crosscut into:
    9 squares, each 1½" x 1½", for sashing squares;

4 strips, each 2" x 42", for inner border.

From the green print, cut:
2 pieces, each 12" x 42", for striped-triangle strip units;

4 squares, each 10" x 10", for bias strip units;

4 strips, each 2½" x 42", for middle border.

From the print for background, cut:
2 pieces, each 12" x 42", for striped-triangle strip units;

5 strips, each 3" x 42", for striped-square strip units.

From the light floral print, cut:
7 strips, each 1½" x 42"; crosscut into:
    24 pieces, each 1½" x 8½", for inner sashing
    strips;

4 strips, each 1½" x 42", for outer sashing strips.

From the fabric for binding, cut:
6 strips, each 2" x 42".

Piecing the Blocks
**Press seam allowances in the direction of
the arrows unless otherwise instructed.**

1. Refer to pages 48–49 for directions to cut
   Method Two bias strips:

Fabric	No. of Pieces	Dimensions	Full Bias Strips from Each Piece	Strip Width
Brick red	2	12" x 42"	12	3"
Green	2	12" x 42"	18	1½"
Background	2	12" x 42"	9	4"

   Set aside the leftover green 12" corner
   pieces for use later. Save the leftover corner
   pieces from other fabrics to use in another
   project.

2. Using the 3" brick red, 1½" green, and 4"
   background strips, assemble 3 striped-triangle
   strip units as shown.

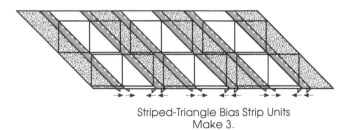

Striped-Triangle Bias Strip Units
Make 3.

3. Position the diagonal line of the Bias Square
   ruler on the green/light seam of the strip unit.
   Cut a total of 32 striped squares, each 4⅞" x
   4⅞", from the strip units. Cut the striped
   squares once diagonally to yield 64 striped
   triangles.

Cut a total
of 32.

4. Using 4¼" x 42" black strips and 3" x 42"
   background strips, make 2 different strip units,
   as shown.

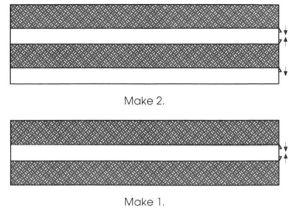

Make 2.

Make 1.

5. Sew the strip units together, offsetting them
   by 2½" as shown. Center the diagonal line of
   the Bias Square ruler over the center of the
   middle strip. Cut 16 center striped squares,
   each 7" x 7", from the strip unit. If needed,
   draw a chalk line through the center of the
   strip, 1¼" from the seam, as a guide.

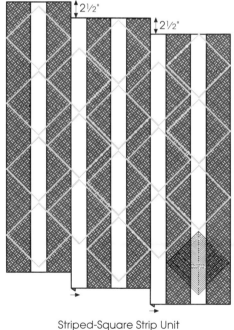

Striped-Square Strip Unit
Make 1.

6. Cut each of the 16 center-striped squares twice
   diagonally to yield 64 side-striped triangles as
   shown.

7. Sew a brick red/green striped triangle from step 3 to each of the 64 side-striped triangles as shown to make 32 units of each type.

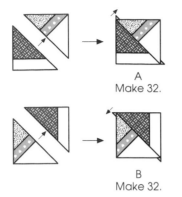

A
Make 32.

B
Make 32.

8. Sew the units into pairs. Make 16 of each half block.

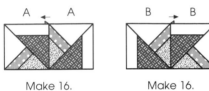

Make 16.   Make 16.

9. Join the half blocks to make 8 of each block. Press the final seam to one side.

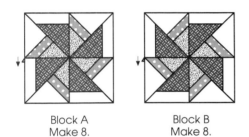

Block A
Make 8.

Block B
Make 8.

Assembling and Finishing the Quilt Top

1. Arrange the blocks and 1½" x 8½" sashing strips into 4 horizontal rows as shown at top right. Alternate the 2 types of blocks within the rows and from row to row. Stitch blocks and sashing together in rows and press seams toward the sashing strips.

2. Make 3 long sashing strips, using 4 inner sashing strips and 3 brick red 1½" squares in each strip.

Make 3.

3. Join the rows of blocks with the pieced sashing strips in between. Press seams toward the sashing strips.

4. Refer to the directions on page 94 for measuring, cutting, and attaching borders with corner squares. Trim the 1½" x 42" floral outer sashing strips to match the center length measurement of the quilt top for the side sashing. Trim the remaining 2 outer sashing strips to match the center width measurement of the quilt top for the top and bottom sashing. Sew the side sashing to the sides of the quilt top; press seams toward the sashing.

5. Cut 4 corner squares, each 1½" x 1½", from leftover floral strips, and sew a square to each end of the top and bottom outer sashing strips; press seams toward the sashing. Sew the strips to the top and bottom of the quilt top; press seams toward the sashing.

6. Measure, trim, and sew the 2" brick red inner border strips as described for the outer sashing strips. Cut 4 corner squares, each 2" x 2", from leftover brick red strips.

7. Measure, trim, and sew the 2½" green middle border strips as described for outer sashing strips. Cut 4 corner squares, each 2½" x 2½", from leftover green strips.

8. Cut 2 black 12" squares once diagonally. With right sides together, pair each 12" black triangle with a 12" green corner piece from step

1 of "Piecing the Blocks." Cut 2½"-wide bias strips from the pairs.

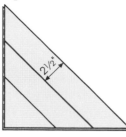

9. Sew 2 bias-strip pairs together along the long edge and then join to make multiple bias strip units. Cut a total of 36 bias squares, each 2½" x 2½", from the strip units.

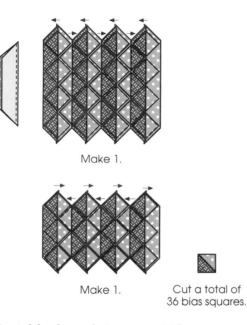

Make 1.

Make 1.   Cut a total of 36 bias squares.

10. Pair 4 black and 4 green 10" squares right sides together and cut in half diagonally. Cut 2½"-wide bias strips and sew multiple bias strip units as in steps 8 and 9. Cut a total of 56 bias squares, each 2½" x 2½", from the strip units.

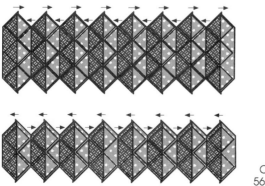

Cut a total of 56 bias squares.

You need a total of 92 bias squares for the pieced border (46 with seams pressed one way and 46 with seams pressed in the other direction).

11. Sew 88 of the bias squares into 44 pairs, using 1 bias square with seams pressed to the black and 1 with seams pressed to the green, so that the diagonal seam intersections butt together.

Make 44 pairs.

12. Make 4 pieced border strips, each with 11 bias-square pairs.

Join 11 pairs.
Make 4 pieced borders.

Note: Before attaching the pieced borders, measure the quilt top. It should measure 44½" x 44½". If it is larger or smaller, the pieced border will not fit. You can ease minor differences by adjusting the seams in the pieced border, making a few of them slightly wider or narrower so the border strips will fit the quilt top.

13. Sew a pieced border to opposite sides of the quilt top with the black points positioned toward the quilt center. Press seams toward the green border.
14. Sew a bias square to each end of the 2 remaining pieced border strips.

15. Sew the pieced borders to the top and bottom of the quilt top, with the black points positioned toward the quilt center. Press seams toward the green border.
16. Cut 1 black 4½" x 42" outer border strip crosswise into 4 pieces, each 4½" x 10". Sew a quarter piece to one end of each of the remaining 42"-long strips. Measure, trim, and sew the black outer border strips as described for previous borders. Cut 4 corner squares, each 4½" x 4½", from leftover black strips.
17. Layer the completed quilt top with batting and backing; baste.
18. Quilt as desired.
19. Bind the edges, following the directions on pages 95–96.

Curves and Diamonds

CUTTING DIAMONDS

This section introduces techniques for cutting and piecing 45°-angle diamonds and for sewing set-in and curved seams.

CUTTING DIAMONDS

Instead of making templates for diamonds, it is a simple process to cut them from strips of fabric. The four sides of a true diamond are equal in length, just as the sides of a square are equal.

To cut diamonds from fabric strips:
1. Cut fabric strips the same width as the height of the diamond, including seam allowances.

Cut fabric strips same width as diamond height.

Note: If the height of the diamond does not measure in ⅛" increments, make a paper template of the desired diamond size with seam allowances added on all four sides. Tape the diamond template to the underside of a see-through acrylic ruler, aligning one side with the edge of the ruler as shown. Use the width of the template as the cutting guide for the fabric strips.

2. Cut the diamonds at a 45° angle from single layers of fabric strips the same width as the diamond. For example, cut a 2⅝" diamond segment from a 2⅝"-wide strip. First, cut a 45° angle at one end of the fabric strip. Then, cut the segments, aligning the 45°-angle line on your ruler with the top or bottom edge of the fabric strip.

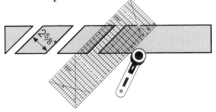

To cut diamonds from pieced strip units, place the 45°-ruler line along one of the interior seams and cut the segments, making the cut at a 45° angle to the interior seams. It is important to cut at an exact 45° angle so that the pieced diamond is not crooked.

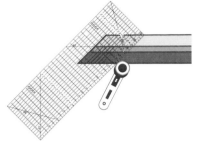

SEWING DIAMONDS

Many quilters are apprehensive about sewing diamond shapes together. Stitching diamonds accurately takes a bit of care and a little practice, but it is really a "toothless dragon." The key is to sew from point to point and to press the seams in a circular fashion so that the seam intersections butt and lie perfectly flat when finished. Add any squares, triangles, or other set-in shapes last. The traditional LeMoyne Star is an example of a block that requires this piecing technique.

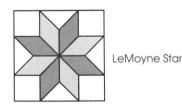

LeMoyne Star

1. Mark the ¼" seam-allowance intersections (the points) on the wrong side of the fabric at all four corners of each diamond.

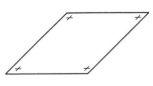

2. Arrange the diamonds for the block in the appropriate color sequence.

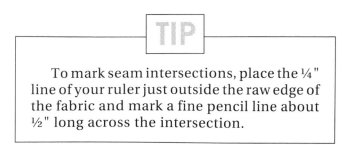

3. Pin the diamonds together in pairs and sew from the center point to the point at the opposite end; backstitch at both points.

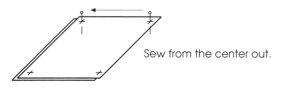

Sew from the center out.

4. Press seams consistently in a clockwise or counterclockwise direction.

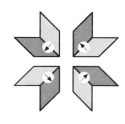

5. Join the diamond pairs to make two star halves. Butt the seams and sew from the center point to the point at the opposite end; backstitch at both points.

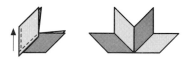

6. Pin the two star halves together, using a pin or partial basting to secure the center point. The seams on each half should butt together, making matching easy. Pin the two outer points securely as well.

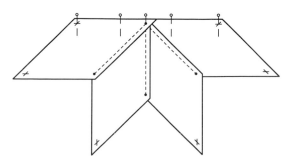

7. Sew the final seam to join the two halves, stitching from one side to the other, point to point. Press in a circular fashion, with the seam allowances forming a rosette, or pinwheel, in the center.

SEWING SET-IN SEAMS

Use set-in seams when the only way to add a piece to a block is by stitching the piece in two stages. Diamond blocks frequently have set-in squares and triangles.

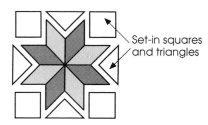

Set-in squares and triangles

1. Mark the ¼" seam intersections on the fabric piece at the inside corner.

2. Begin by pinning one side of the seam; match the corners exactly. If necessary, fold or pin any pressed seams out of the way.
3. Begin by backstitching in the corner and stitch from the inside corner to the outer edge.

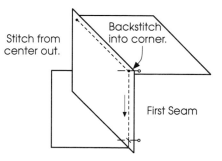

Stitch from center out.

Backstitch into corner.

First Seam

4. Beginning at the inside corner, pin the other side of the seam and sew from the inside corner to the outer edge. Be careful not to catch the other seam or seam allowance when stitching the second side.

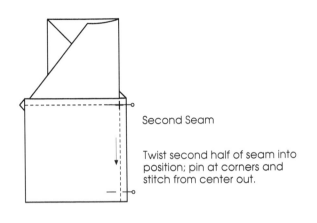

Second Seam

Twist second half of seam into position; pin at corners and stitch from center out.

SEWING CURVED SEAMS

Every curved seam has two types of curves: convex and concave. When matching these two curves, notice that they are mirror images, and the concave seam must be "stretched" to fit the convex seam.

1. Mark the centers of both curves.

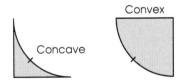

Convex

Concave

2. To create a smooth seam, clip periodically into the concave seam allowance. There is no need to clip the convex seam. Clip no farther than ⅛" into the seam allowance. It is better to put only a few clips into the seam at first and add more later, if necessary.

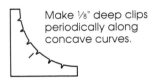

Make ⅛" deep clips periodically along concave curves.

3. Place pins in the outer raw edges to keep the edges from slipping out of position. Pin at the center, matching the center guidelines. Place additional pins around the curve as you ease the seams together.

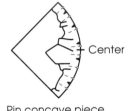

Center

Pin concave piece to convex piece with center guidelines matching.

4. Stitch the seam slowly and carefully from one raw edge to the other. Remove any pins from the seam as you stitch; press the seam toward the concave piece.

Warm-up

PROJECT

Day in the Garden

Finished Size: 35⅛" x 46⅜"

Finished Block Size: 7"

Color photos on page 30

There are two block versions of this quilt pattern in these directions. If you study the two blocks closely, you will notice that one version has a curved bud while the other has a straight-pieced bud.

Materials: 44"-wide fabric
⅞ yd. plum floral print
⅜ yd. burgundy
⅛ yd. medium green
⅜ yd. dark green
1 yd. for background
⅜ yd. periwinkle blue for sashing
⅜ yd. for binding
1½ yds. for backing

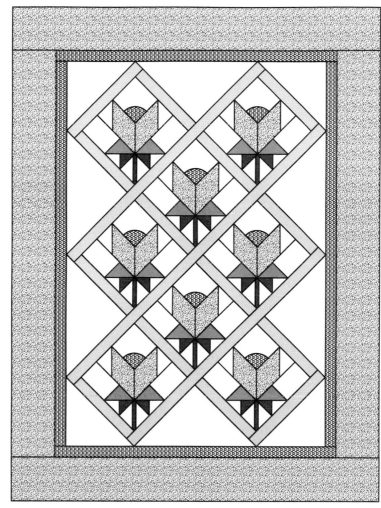

Color Key
- Plum floral
- Burgundy
- Medium green
- Dark green
- Background
- Periwinkle blue

Tulip A
Curved Bud
Make 8.

OR

Tulip B
Square Bud
Make 8.

Cutting: All measurements include ¼"-wide seam allowances. *Use templates on page 93.*

From the plum floral print, cut:
2 strips, each 2⅝" x 42", for diamonds;

4 strips, each 4½" x 42", for outer border.

From the burgundy fabric, cut:
8 Template A, for tulip buds, Version A*;

4 strips, each 2" x 42", for inner border.

From the medium green, cut:
1 strip, 2¾" x 42"; crosscut into:
    8 squares, each 2¾" x 2¾", for sepals (calyx).

*If you make tulips with pointed buds instead of curved ones, eliminate Template A and cut 1 strip, 2" x 20".

From the dark green, cut:
1 piece, 8" x 12", for bias strip unit;

1 piece, 6" x 11", for striped-square strip unit.

From the background fabric, cut:
1 piece, 8" x 42"; crosscut into:
    1 piece, 8" x 12", for bias strip unit;
    1 piece, 6" x 22", for striped-square strip unit;
    4 squares, each 3" x 3", for blocks;

1 piece, 12¾" x 42"; crosscut into:
    2 squares, each 12¾" x 12¾", for side setting
      triangles;
    2 squares, each 7½" x 7½", for corner
      triangles;

1 strip, 3¾" x 42"; crosscut into:
    16 bars, each 2⅜" x 3¾", for blocks;

1 strip, 3½" x 42"; crosscut into:
    8 Template B**, for bud units, Version A;
    4 squares, each 3" x 3", for block piecing.

From the periwinkle blue for the sashing, cut:
5 strips, each 1½" x 42"; crosscut into:
    1 strip, 1½" x 33½";
    2 strips, each 1½" x 25½";
    2 strips, each 1½" x 9½";
    12 strips, each 1½" x 7½".

From the fabric for binding, cut:
4 strips, each 2" x 42".

    **If you make tulips with pointed buds instead
of curved ones, eliminate Template B and cut 2
strips, each 2" x 42"; crosscut into 1 strip, 2" x 20",
and 8 bars, each 2" x 3½".

Piecing the Blocks
**Press seam allowances in the direction of
the arrows unless otherwise instructed.**

1. Cut 2 plum floral 2⅝" x 42" strips into 16
   diamonds, each 2⅝". Place the 45° line of
   your ruler on the top edge of the fabric to cut
   the segments at the correct angle.

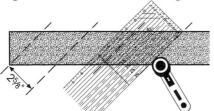

2. Cut the 3" background squares once diagonally to yield 16 half-square triangles.

3. Sew 1 half-square triangle to the upper right
   side of 8 diamonds and 1 half-square triangle
   to the upper left side of 8 diamonds.

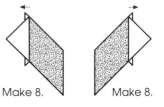

Make 8.   Make 8.

4. Mark the seam intersections with cross-hair
   marks on the upper inside corners as shown.
   Sew the left and right diamonds into pairs,
   matching the marks and pinning. Stitch from
   the marks toward the raw edge. Remember to
   backstitch.

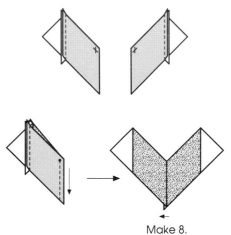

Make 8.

Note: If you are making Version A with the curved
bud, continue with step 5 and skip step 6. If
you are making the pointed bud, Version B,
skip step 5 and proceed to step 6.

5. For curved buds, sew the Template A pieces
   to the Template B pieces, aligning the edges
   and the center marks; clip the Template B
   pieces as necessary.

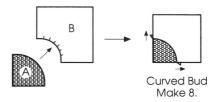

Curved Bud
Make 8.

6. For pointed buds, sew the 2" x 20" burgundy
   and background strips together; press seams
   toward the background fabric. Cut 8 segments,
   each 2" wide, from the strip unit. Sew each
   segment to a 2" x 3½" background bar. Press
   seams toward the bars.

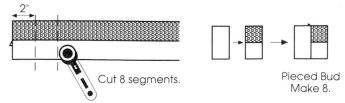

Cut 8 segments.

Pieced Bud
Make 8.

7. On the back of each burgundy bud (whether straight or curved), mark the seam intersection with cross-hair lines. Using a set-in seam (pages 81–82), join the bud piece between the 2 diamonds, matching the marks and pinning. Sew each half of the set-in seam separately, stitching from the center out toward the raw edges. Press seams toward the diamonds.

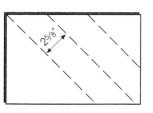

Cross-hair lines

8. With right sides together, cut the 8" x 12" dark green and background pieces into 2⅝"-wide bias strips, including 1 corner piece. Reserve left-over corner pieces for another project.

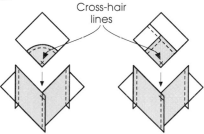

2⅝"

9. Assemble a bias strip unit as shown. Cut 8 bias squares, each 2¾" x 2¾", from the strip unit.

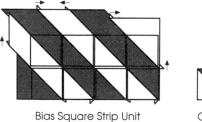

Bias Square Strip Unit   Cut 8.

10. Cut the bias squares in half diagonally to yield 16 side-by-side triangles.

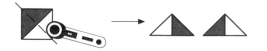

11. Cut the medium green 2¾" squares once diagonally to yield 16 half-square triangles. Sew 1 medium green triangle to each of the 16 side-by-side triangles to create 2 leaf-unit versions as shown. You will need 1 of each version for a block.

Make 8.   Make 8.

12. Sew a 2⅜" x 3¾" bar of background fabric to the medium green side of each leaf unit as shown. Carefully position the leaf units as shown before sewing.

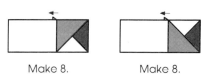

Make 8.   Make 8.

13. Cut the dark green 6" x 11" piece into 4 full bias strips, each ⅞" wide. Cut the background 6" x 22" piece into 5 full bias strips, each 2¼" wide. Set the 7" corner triangles aside to use in another project.

14. Assemble a bias strip unit as shown. Center the diagonal line of the Bias Square ruler in the center of the dark green strip, and cut 8 striped squares, each 2⅜" x 2⅜".

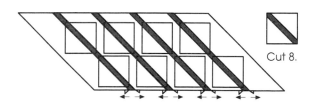

Cut 8.

15. Arrange the tulip and leaf units as shown and stitch. Be sure to use the correct leaf unit.

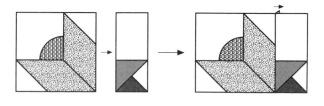

16. Carefully position the striped squares (stems) and the remaining leaf units as shown and stitch.

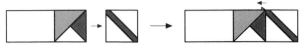

Make 8.

17. Sew the leaf/stem unit to the tulip sections to complete the block.

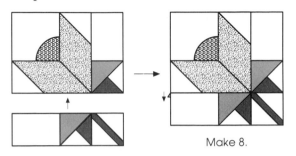

Make 8.

Assembling and Finishing the Quilt Top

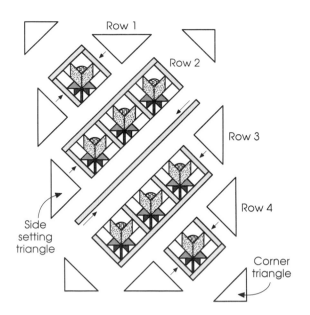

Row 1
Row 2
Row 3
Row 4
Side setting triangle
Corner triangle

1. Cut the 12¾" background squares twice diagonally to yield 8 side setting triangles. Cut the 7½" background square once diagonally to yield 4 corner triangles.

2. Arrange the Tulip blocks, sashing strips, and corner and side setting triangles in diagonal rows as shown in the setting diagram at top right. Sew the blocks and short sashing strips together in rows. Press seams toward the sashing.

3. Add the 1½" x 9½" sashing strips to rows 1 and 4, then add the side setting triangles at each row end.

4. Add the 1½" x 25½" sashing strips to rows 2 and 3, then add a side setting triangle to the end of each row.

5. Sew rows 1 and 2 together and rows 3 and 4 together.

6. Sew the 1½" x 33½" sashing piece to a quilt-top half, stitching in the direction of the arrow. Add the other quilt-top half, stitching in the opposite direction. Press seams toward the sashing.

7. Sew the corner triangles to the quilt top last; press seams toward the triangles.

8. Square up the corners of the quilt top with your ruler, trimming the quilt sides to within ¼" of the sashing points. (See page 94.)

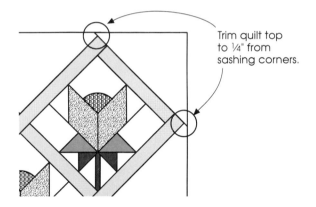

Trim quilt top to ¼" from sashing corners.

9. Refer to the directions on page 94 for measuring, cutting, and attaching borders with straight-cut corners. Trim 2 of the burgundy 2" x 42" inner border strips to match the center length measurement of the quilt top and sew to opposite sides; press seams toward the border. Trim the other 2 burgundy inner border strips to match the center width measurement of the quilt top and sew to the top and bottom; press seams toward the border.

10. Measure, cut, and sew the 4½"-wide plum floral outer border strips to the quilt top as described for the inner border.

11. Layer the completed quilt top with batting and backing; baste.

12. Quilt as desired.

13. Bind the edges, following the directions on pages 95–96.

Glory of the Season

Finished Size: 41" x 47"

Finished Block Size: 6"

Color photo on page 32

Six diamonds are sewn together to form each Leaf Block in this quilt pattern, making it a little more intricate than "Day in the Garden" on pages 83–86. There are two types of blocks with appliquéd curved stems. Directions for bias stems are included, but you may substitute ³⁄₁₆"-wide satin ribbon instead. Although this quilt pattern requires one brown print for the tree trunks, you may add interest by using several brown prints from your scrap bag.

Materials: 44"-wide fabric

⅜ yd. each of 6 assorted autumn prints

1⅜ yds. light blue

¼ yd. brown for tree trunks and stems*

⅜ yd. red-orange for inner border

½ yd. brown for middle border

½ yd. green for outer border

2⅞ yds. of ³⁄₁₆"-wide satin ribbon* (optional)

⅜ yd. for binding

1½ yds. for backing

*If you use satin ribbon for leaf stems, you only need ⅛ yd. fabric for the tree trunks.

Color Key

- Yellow
- Red-orange
- Rust
- Green
- Brown
- Light blue

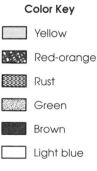

Block A
Make 10.

Block B
Make 10.

Cutting: All measurements include ¼"-wide seam allowances.

From each of the 6 assorted autumn prints, cut:
1 piece, 6" x 16", for Strip Unit I;

4 strips, each 1¾" x 25", for diamonds.

From the light blue, cut:
3 strips, each 6" x 42"; crosscut into:
  6 pieces, each 6" x 16", for Strip Unit I;

2 strips, each 3¾" x 42"; crosscut into:
  18 squares, each 3¾" x 3¾", for Blocks A and B;

3 strips, each 1¾" x 42"; crosscut into:
  6 strips, each 1¾" x 21", for Strip Unit II;

1 strip, 5⅛" x 42"; crosscut into:
  5 squares, each 5⅛" x 5⅛", for Block B,
  4 squares, each 2½" x 2½", for pieced border corners;

5 strips, each 2¼" x 42"; crosscut into:
  50 squares, each 2¼" x 2¼", for Blocks A and B;
  10 bars, each 2¼" x 6½", for Block A.

From the brown for tree trunks and stems, cut:
2 strips, each 1" x 42"; crosscut into:
  3 strips, each 1" x 21", for Strip Unit II;

1 strip, 4" x 42", for bias stems. You don't need to cut these stems if you are using satin ribbon.

From the red-orange for inner border, cut:
4 strips, each 2" x 42".

From the brown for middle border, cut:
4 strips, each 3½" x 42".

From the green for outer border, cut:
5 strips*, each 2½" x 42".

From the fabric for binding, cut:
5 strips, each 2" x 42".

*If your fabric measures 43½" wide after washing and removing the selvages, cut only 4 strips.

Piecing the Blocks
Press seam allowances in the direction of the arrows unless otherwise instructed.

1. Cut the 1¾" x 25" autumn print strips into 45° diamonds at 1¾" intervals. Cut 18 diamonds from 4 of the prints, and 24 diamonds from the remaining 2 prints. Sort the diamonds into 20 groups, with 6 diamonds of the same print in each.

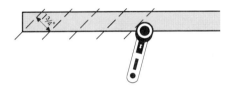

2. Mark backs of diamonds at each seam intersection with cross hairs.

3. Referring to "Sewing Diamonds" on pages 80–81, sew the diamonds into pairs. Join the pairs to make a 6-diamond leaf unit.

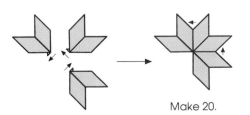

Make 20.

4. Cut 18 blue 3¾" squares twice diagonally to yield 72 quarter-square triangles. Mark cross hairs at the seam intersections on the quarter-square triangles and on each blue 2¼" square as shown.

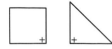

5. Choose which 6-diamond leaf units will be used for Block A and which will be used for Block B. You will make 10 of each type. Distribute colors and values evenly between the 2 types of blocks.

6. Using a set-in seam, join the 2¼" blue squares and quarter-square triangles from step 4 to Block A, and Block B, as shown. Press seams counterclockwise. Save the remaining quarter-square triangles for step 8.

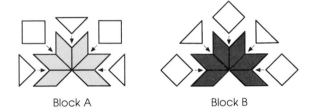

Block A   Block B

7. Cut the 4" x 42" brown stem strip into 20 bias strips, each ¾" wide. Fold each bias stem in half, wrong sides together, along the long edges. Stitch the raw edges together with a ¼"-wide seam, making a small bias tube. Trim the seam to ⅛" and press the stem flat, with the seam centered on the back of the tube. If you are using 3/16"-wide satin ribbon for the stems instead, cut the ribbon into 20 pieces, each 5" long.

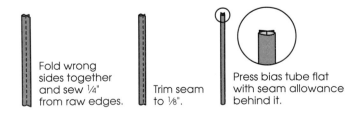

Fold wrong sides together and sew ¼" from raw edges.   Trim seam to ⅛".   Press bias tube flat with seam allowance behind it.

8. Partially appliqué a stem to each of 20 blue quarter-square triangles as shown, leaving part of it unstitched and allowing the top of the stem to extend ¼" past the raw edge of the triangle corner.

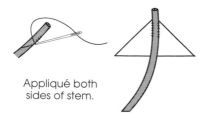

Appliqué both
sides of stem.

9. Using a set-in seam, sew the triangles with the partially appliquéd stems to each Block A and Block B leaf unit as shown. Press seams toward the diamonds. Trim the excess stem at the point behind the center diamond.

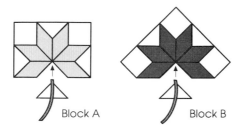

Block A　　　　Block B

10. Sew a 2¼" x 6½" blue bar to each Block A. Fold the stem out of the way while stitching.

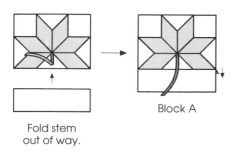

Block A

Fold stem
out of way.

11. Cut 5 blue 5⅛" squares once diagonally to yield 10 half-square triangles. Sew a half-square triangle to each Block B. Fold the stem out of the way while stitching. Trim the excess stem length at the point behind the diamond center.

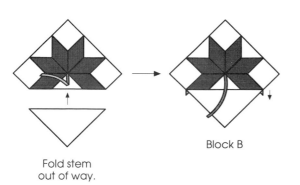

Block B

Fold stem
out of way.

12. Finish appliquéing the stems to complete the blocks. The stem may be curved in any direction. Leave about ¼" to ½" excess stem extending beyond the raw edge of the block.

Assembling and Finishing the Quilt Top

1. Arrange the blocks into 5 rows of 4 blocks each, referring to the quilt plan on page 87 for placement. Sew the blocks together in horizontal rows. Press seams in opposite directions from row to row. Trim the excess stem fabric from the seams.

2. Refer to the directions on page 94 for measuring, cutting, and attaching borders with straight-cut corners. Trim 2 of the red-orange 2" x 42" inner border strips to match the center length measurement of the quilt top and sew to the sides; press seams toward the border.

3. Trim the other 2 red-orange inner border strips to match the center width measurement of the quilt top and sew to the top and bottom; press seams toward the border.

4. Measure, trim, and sew the 3½" brown middle border strips to the quilt top as described for the inner border.

5. With right sides facing up, pair each 6" x 16" autumn print with a 6" x 16" blue piece. Cut the pairs into 2¼"-wide bias strips (including corner pieces), following the directions on pages 48–49 for cutting Method Two bias strips.

6. Assemble 6 Strip Unit I, one for each autumn print, as shown. Cut 16 bias squares, each 2" x 2", from each Strip Unit I.

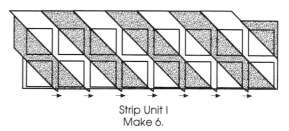

Strip Unit I
Make 6.

7. For treetops, sew 16 bias squares from each color combination into 8 pairs, using 1 bias square with seams pressed toward the blue and 1 bias square with seams pressed toward the autumn print. You should have a total of 48 treetops in assorted autumn prints.

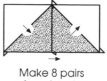

Make 8 pairs
of each color.

8. Using 1¾" x 21" blue strips and 1" x 21" brown strips, assemble 3 of Strip Unit II as shown. Cut a total of 48 segments, each 1" wide, from the strip units for the tree trunks.

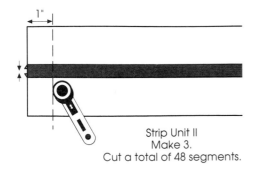

Strip Unit II
Make 3.
Cut a total of 48 segments.

9. Sew a tree trunk to the base of each tree. Arrange the trees randomly to make 2 pieced border strips of 11 trees each for the top and bottom borders, and 2 pieced border strips of 13 trees each for the sides. Press seams joining tree trunks to tree tops in opposite directions from tree to tree so seams butt when joining trees. Stitch together; press seams to one side. Sew a 2½" blue square to each end of the top and bottom border strips; press seams toward the blue squares.

10. Positioning the tree strips as shown in the quilt plan, sew a pieced border strip with 13 trees to opposite sides of the quilt top; press seams toward the middle border.

11. Sew a pieced border strip with 11 trees to the top and bottom of the quilt top; press seams toward the middle border.

12. If your green outer border strips measure 43½" long, you need 4 strips. If border strips measure less than 43½", cut 1 of the 5 green 2½" x 42" strips in half crosswise. Sew a half strip to one end of 2 of the 42"-long strips for the side borders. Measure, cut, and sew the side, top, and bottom border strips as described for the inner border.

13. Layer the completed quilt top with batting and backing; baste.

14. Quilt as desired.

15. Bind the edges, following the directions on pages 95–96.

Make 2 for top and bottom.

Make 2 for sides.

Starbloom

Finished Size: 43" x 43"

Finished Block Size: 14½"

Color photo on page 31

This is a glorious quilt pattern. Make it in deep, rich colors; lovely pastels; or even warm plaids. The size of the blocks makes Starbloom a good candidate for a bed-sized quilt. This quilt is the most challenging of the diamond patterns, with eight pieced diamonds required for each block.

Materials: 44"-wide fabric

¾ yd. dark pink

¼ yd. each of medium pink, light pink, dark green, and light green

⅜ yd. background fabric

¾ yd. print for outer border

2¾ yds. for backing

⅜ yd. for binding

Color Key

- Dark pink
- Medium pink
- Light pink
- Dark green
- Light green
- Background

Starbloom
Make 4.

Cutting: All measurements include ¼"-wide seam allowances.

From the dark red, cut:
4 strips, each 1¼" x 42", for diamond strip unit;

1 strip, each 5⅛" x 42"; crosscut into:
    8 squares, each 5⅛" x 5⅛", for block corners;

4 strips, each 2½" x 42", for inner border.

From the medium red, cut:
4 strips, each 1¼" x 42", for diamond strip unit.

From the light red, cut:
4 strips, each 1⅛" x 42", for diamond strip unit.

From the dark green, cut:
32 Template C.

From the medium green, cut:
32 Template D.

From the background fabric, cut:
4 strips, each 2⅝" x 42", for plain diamonds.

From the outer border print, cut:
4 strips, each 5½" x 42".

From the fabric for binding, cut:
5 strips, each 2" x 42".

Piecing the Blocks

Press seam allowances in the direction of the arrows unless otherwise instructed.

1. Sew 4 strip units as shown, using a 1¼" x 42" dark red and a medium red strip and a 1⅛" x 42" light red strip. Offset the strips by 1" when sewing. Press all seams toward the light strip.

Offset by 1" and press toward light strip.

Make 4.

2. Cut a total of 32 striped diamonds from the strip units at a 45° angle, each 2⅝" wide.

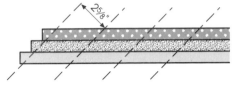

Cut a total of 32 striped diamonds.

3. Mark cross hairs at each seam intersection of each diamond on wrong side of diamond unit.

4. Referring to "Sewing Diamonds" on pages 80–81, sew the diamonds into pairs.

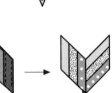

5. Join pairs into halves.

6. Join the halves to make 4 striped diamond stars.

7. Referring to "Sewing Curved Seams" on page 82, sew Template C to Template D.

8. Mark cross hairs at the seam intersections on the wrong side of the pieced unit.

9. Using a set-in seam (pages 81–82), sew a curved unit to each diamond pair as shown. Sew from point to point. Press set-in seams counterclockwise.

10. Cut each 2⅝" x 42" background strip into 2⅝" segments at a 45° angle, to yield a total of 32 diamonds.

Cut a total of 32 diamonds.

11. Mark cross hairs at the seam intersections on the wrong side of the background-fabric diamonds.

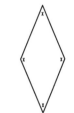

12. Using set-in seams, sew the background-fabric diamonds to the center unit as shown. Stitch in the direction of the arrows. Press seams counterclockwise.

13. Cut 8 dark red 5⅛" squares once diagonally to yield 16 half-square triangles. Sew 1 triangle to each corner of each Starbloom block. Press seams toward the red triangles.

Assembling and Finishing the Quilt Top

1. Join the 4 Starbloom blocks together into pairs. Press the seams in each pair open for a flat intersection. Join the pairs to complete the quilt center. Press the final seam open.

2. Refer to the directions on page 94 for measuring, cutting, and attaching borders with corner squares to the quilt top. Trim 2 of the dark red 2½" x 42" inner border strips to match the center length measurement of the quilt top for side borders. Trim the other 2 dark red inner border strips to match the center width measurement of the quilt top for top and bottom borders. Sew side borders to the quilt top; press seams toward the border.

3. Cut 4 corner squares, each 2½" x 2½", from leftover dark red strips, and sew a square to each end of the 2 remaining border strips; press seams toward the border. Sew the border strips to the top and bottom of the quilt top; press seams toward the border.

4. Measure, trim, and sew the 5½"-wide outer border strips as described for the inner border. Cut corner squares, each 5½" x 5½", from leftover outer border strips.

5. Layer the completed quilt top with batting and backing; baste.

6. Quilt as desired.

7. Bind the edges, following the directions on pages 95–96.

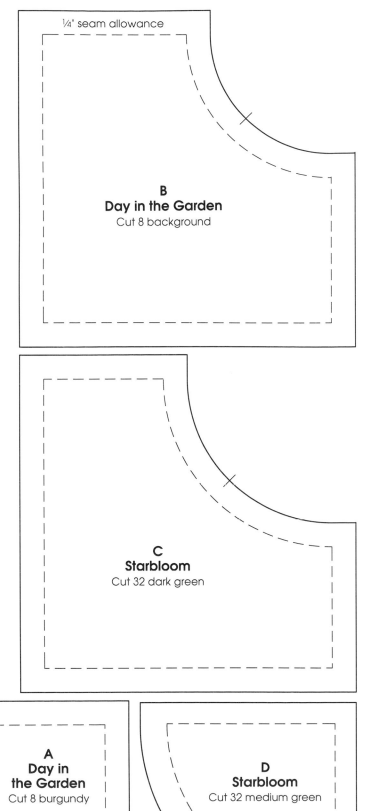

¼" seam allowance

B
Day in the Garden
Cut 8 background

C
Starbloom
Cut 32 dark green

A
Day in the Garden
Cut 8 burgundy

D
Starbloom
Cut 32 medium green

Finishing

Once you have completed the blocks, you'll be anxious to finish the entire quilt. Assembly instructions are included with each quilt pattern in this book, but here are a few additional tips for finishing that you may find useful.

BORDERS

Straighten the edges of the quilt top before adding the borders. There should be little or no trimming needed for a straight-set quilt. A diagonally set quilt is often constructed with oversized side setting triangles (page 9), and you may need to trim these down to size. Align the ¼" line on the ruler with the block points and trim the quilt edges to ¼" from these points. Always position a ruler along the block points of the adjacent edge

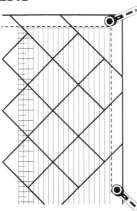

Trim the edges of the quilt to ¼" from the block points, using a ruler to square the corners.

at the same time, so that the corner will be square when the trimming has been completed.

To find the correct measurement for plain border strips, always measure through the center of the quilt, not at the outside edges. This ensures that the borders are of equal length on opposite sides of the quilt and brings the outer edges into line with the center dimension if discrepancies exist. Otherwise, your quilt might not be "square," due to minor piecing errors and/or stretching that can occur while you work with the pieces.

Straight-cut borders run from one side of the quilt to the other, without a corner square. Corner squares are separate squares of fabric that join two adjacent side borders at the corners. Each of these border types is measured differently.

For borders with straight-cut corners:

1. Measure the quilt from the top to the bottom edge through the center of the quilt. Cut two of the border strips to this measurement and pin them to the sides of the quilt, easing or slightly stretching the quilt top to fit the border strip as necessary.

Center length

Note: If there is a large difference in the two sides, it is better to go back and correct the source of the problem now rather than try to make the border fit and end up with a distorted quilt later.

2. Sew the side borders in place and press the seams toward the borders.

3. Measure the center width of the quilt, including the side borders, to determine the length of the top and bottom border strips. Cut the borders to this measurement and pin them to the top and bottom of the

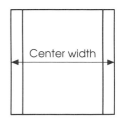

Center width

quilt top, again easing or slightly stretching the quilt to fit as needed. Stitch in place and press the seams toward the border strips.

For borders with corner squares:

1. Measure the width and length of the quilt top through the center. Cut border strips to those measurements, piecing as necessary.

2. Pin the side borders to opposite sides of the quilt top, matching centers and ends and easing as necessary. Sew the side border strips; press seams toward the border.

3. Cut corner squares of the required size (the cut width of the border strips). Sew one corner square to each end of the remaining two border strips; press seams toward the border strips. Pin the border strips to the top and bottom edges of the quilt top, matching centers, seams between the border strip and corner square, and ends, easing as necessary.

4. Sew the top and bottom border strips with corner squares to the quilt. Press seams toward the border.

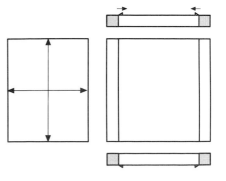

After adding borders, you are ready to prepare the quilt top for quilting. You'll find complete directions for this step and for hand quilting in the "Joy of Quilting" companion book *Loving Stitches* by Jeana Kimball.

BINDING

The fabric requirements for the patterns in this book are based on cutting straight-of-grain fabric strips for a double-fold binding. This is a simple but durable binding. Cut 2"-wide strips from selvage to selvage for a standard ¼"-wide finished binding.

When the binding strips are joined together, they may be seamed with either a vertical or a diagonal seam, but a diagonal seam is less noticeable. To create a diagonal seam, lay the two strips, right sides together, at right angles to each other; pin. Seam them from corner to corner as shown. Cut away the excess at the outer corner and press the seam open to reduce bulk. It is important to use closely matching threads in this situation to avoid peekaboo stitches at the seams.

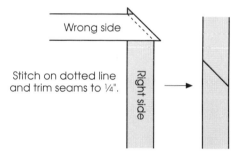

Once all the strips are sewn together into a continuous piece of binding, press the strip in half lengthwise, wrong sides together.

To attach the binding:
1. Trim the batting and the backing even with the quilt-top edges. True up the edges and corners if necessary.
2. Baste the three layers of the quilt securely at the outer edges if you have removed all previous basting.

3. In the center of one edge of the quilt, align the raw edges of the binding with the raw edge of the quilt top. Leaving about 6"–8" free as a starting tail, sew the binding to the edge of the quilt with a ¼"-wide seam allowance. Stop stitching ¼" from the corner of the first side. (It's a good idea to pin-mark ¼" in from the corner before you begin sewing.) Backstitch and remove the quilt from the machine.

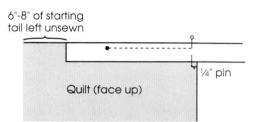

4. To create a neat, mitered turn at the corner, flip the binding straight up from the corner so that it forms a continuous line with the adjacent side of the quilt top.

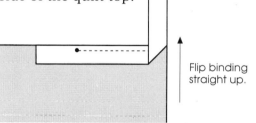

5. Fold the binding straight down so that it lies on top of the adjacent side, being careful not to shift the pleat formed at the fold. Pin the pleat in place. Pin-mark ¼" in from the next corner. Starting at the edge, stitch the second side of the binding to the quilt, stopping at the ¼" mark. Flip up, then down, repeating the same process for the remaining corners.

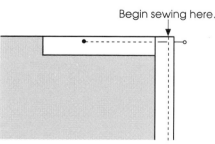

6. After turning the fourth corner, stitch to within 8" of the starting tail. Cut the two tails so that they overlap by about 3"–4". If the seams are vertical, cut the ending tail to ½" larger than the starting tail; seam the two right sides together with a ¼" seam. Press the seam open.

Note: If the seams on your binding are diagonal, use a diagonal seam to join the two tails together. Open the two tails so they are no longer folded in half. Lay the ending tail under the starting tail and draw a diagonal line to match the diagonal cut of the starting tail. Cut the ending tail ½" longer than this line.

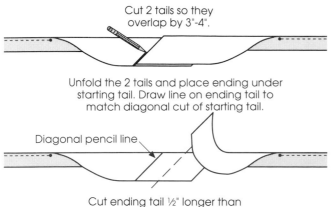

Cut 2 tails so they overlap by 3"-4".

Unfold the 2 tails and place ending under starting tail. Draw line on ending tail to match diagonal cut of starting tail.

Diagonal pencil line

Cut ending tail ½" longer than diagonal pencil line.

Join the tails together, offsetting them as shown; press open.

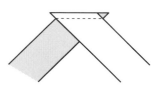

7. Refold the binding and lay it back in place along the edge of the quilt. It should be a perfect fit. Stitch the remaining length of binding in place.
8. Turn the binding to the back of the quilt. Slipstitch the fold of the binding to the quilt back. Slipstitch the miters in place on both the front and back to complete the binding—and your quilt!

Donna Thomas made her first quilt—a gift for her husband-to-be—while she was a student at Penn State in 1975. That was just the beginning of her love affair with quilting, although she has sewn all her life. She taught her first quilting class in 1982 and has been teaching ever since, earning her National Quilting Association certification in 1988. After four years in Germany, teaching and writing, Donna now lives with her husband and two sons in Lansing, Kansas, where she continues to teach, write, and pursue her other passion—gardening.

Donna is the author of *Small Talk*, a book on miniature quiltmaking, and *A Perfect Match*, on machine piecing. Her best-selling classic, *Shortcuts: A Concise Guide to Rotary Cutting*, has been translated into four languages and is also available in a metric version. She is a contributing author to *The Quilters' Companion: Everything You Need to Know to Make Beautiful Quilts*.